Series/Number 07-123

SOCIAL CHOICE: THEORY AND RESEARCH

PAUL E. JOHNSON
University of Kansas

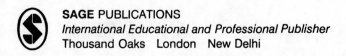

SAGE PUBLICATIONS
International Educational and Professional Publisher
Thousand Oaks   London   New Delhi

For information:

SAGE Publications Ltd
1 Oliver's Yard
55 City Road
London EC1Y 1SP

SAGE Publications Inc.
2455 Teller Road
Thousand Oaks, California 91320

SAGE Publications India Pvt Ltd
B-42, Panchsheel Enclave
Post Box 4109
New Delhi 110 017

Printed in the United States of America

Library of Congress Cataloging-in-Publication Data

Johnson, P. E. (Paul E.)
    Social choice: theory and research / Paul E. Johnson.
        p. cm. — (Quantitative applications in the social sciences;
  vol. 123)
    Includes bibliographical references (p.).
    ISBN 0-7619-1406-4 (pbk.: alk. paper)
    1. Social choice—Mathematical models. 2. Decision-making—
Mathematical models. I. Title. II. Series: Sage university
papers series. Quantitative applications in the social sciences;
07-123.
  HB846.8.J65 1998
  302'.13—dc21   98-20634

This book is printed on acid-free paper.

98 99 00 01 02 03 10 9 8 7 6 5 4 3 2 1

Acquiring Editor:	C. Deborah Laughton
Editorial Assistant:	Eileen Carr
Production Editor:	Astrid Virding
Editorial Assistant:	Nevair Kabakian
Designer/Typesetter:	Technical Typesetting, Inc.

When citing a university paper, please use the proper form. Remember to cite the Sage University Paper series title and incude the paper number. One of the following formats can be adapted (depending on the style manual used):

(1) JOHNSON, P. E. (1998). *Social Choice: Theory and Research.* Sage University Papers Series on Quantitative Applications in the Social Sciences, 07-123. Thousand Oaks, CA: Sage.

OR

(2) Johnson, P. E. (1998). *Social choice: Theory and research* (Sage University Papers Series on Quantitative Application in the Social Sciences, series no. 07-123). Thousand Oaks, CA: Sage.

CONTENTS

SERIES EDITOR'S INTRODUCTION

Social choice theory and research examines the rules for making collective decisions, from the aggregation of individual preferences. What are the rules? Are they fair and logical? Do they result in the optimal outcome? Groups—organizations, corporations, legislatures, committees—have formal rules for the allocation of their resources. In democratic societies, the "gold standard" of decision-making is simple majority rule, where the members of the group express their individual preferences in a vote. However, does this majority rule always improve social well-being? May it sometimes, in fact, lead to collective irrationality? Such provocative questions motivated Professor Johnson's engrossing exposition of a fundamental subject in the formal research domain.

Consider a simple example, illustrating the "voter's paradox." Suppose the University Speaker Committee, composed of three students (Alice, Brenda, and Chris) needs to select one political speaker from a list of three (a Radical, a Liberal, and a Conservative). They must decide by majority rule, voting on the candidates two-at-a-time. Here are their underlying ordered preferences, from most preferred to least:

Alice: Liberal, Radical, Conservative
Brenda: Conservative, Liberal, Radical
Chris: Radical, Conservative, Liberal

Alice, the committee chair, calls a vote on the Liberal–Radical pair, and the Liberal wins with two votes from Alice and Brenda. However, Chris, who really does not like the Liberal, objects and asks for a vote between the Radical and the Conservative. In this pairing, the Radical wins the majority, with Chris's vote and a vote from Alice. Brenda, whose first-choice Conservative preference has been shut out, demands that heads be counted again. To be fair, the committee chair allows a run-off between the Conservative and the Liberal, who had won the first ballot. In this contest, the Conservative actually captures the majority, with votes from Brenda and Chris. The dilemma is clear. Since each of the candidates can command a majority, the committee is locked in a voting cycle. The majority rule here always produces a winner that will be objected to by another majority, and in that sense is not socially preferred.

The problem of aggregating individual preferences into desirable collective decisions received general treatment by Nobel Prize winner Kenneth Arrow. His results suggested that no social welfare function could be derived from even simple rules of democratic decision-making. Johnson carefully goes over Arrow's proof of his "possibility theorem," along the way providing a good introduction to formal method. Further, challenges to the proof are evaluated. For instance, one way out comes from the idea of a Condorcet winner, one capable of beating all rivals. Professor Arrow's work represents discrete social choice models, in contrast to spatial models posing continuous sets of alternatives.

In a unidimensional spatial model, alternatives are drawn from a real number line, e.g., the amount of dollars to be allocated for speakers. The voter has preferences, expressed formally in a utility function. Single-peaked preferences, which in the unidimensional case simply mean that a voter has a favorite, are not so easily defined in the multidimensional model, where the "preferred-to set is a convex set." Professor Johnson elucidates the "convex set" concept, and usefully admonishes the reader to "not gloss over it at this stage." Throughout, his qualities as a teacher shine. At just the right points, he unobtrusively unpacks the mathematical, symbolic, and geometric language. Experienced formalists will appreciate the fineness of his exposition, as much as beginning students will appreciate its clarity. This surpassing monograph seems bound to become a standard primer.

—*Michael S. Lewis-Beck*
Series Editor

ACKNOWLEDGMENTS

I would like to thank my professors at Washington University in St. Louis for the wonderful learning experience they provided. I consider myself lucky to have studied social choice with, in chronological order, William Riker, Kenneth Shepsle, Randy Calvert, Gary Cox, Art Denzau, Gary Miller, and Norman Schofield. My advisor, Robert Salisbury, was always supportive of my desire to integrate formal theory with my research on interest group politics.

I also would like to thank the many students, both undergraduate and graduate, and colleagues who have read earlier versions of this manuscript and provided feedback. Special thanks to Ron Francisco, Steve Garrison, Phil Huxtable, Gary Reich, and Andy Rutton for their feedback. Two reviewers, Kaare Strom at the University of California, San Diego and Charles Tien at Hunter College, pointed out room for improvement in the manuscript.

While it is commonplace to say that all remaining mistakes are the fault of the author, I suppose most authors don't mean it. They really think editors deserve the blame. In this case, however, Mike Lewis-Beck was extremely helpful and encouraging, and the team assembled by Sage to prepare the manuscript did a highly professional job. I only mention this because I was surprised several times by the high quality of the editorial and production staffs. While the last chores in stapling figures and text together are not easy, that group made it comparatively pleasant and methodical.

PREFACE

Not long ago, I received a research paper in the mail that began as follows (Schofield, 1994, p. 1):

> Introduction. The core of a (non-collegial) voting game on a compact policy space W in non-empty only for a nowhere dense set of preferences, where preferences are continuous and endowed with the closed convergence or C^0-topology: that is emptiness of the voting core is generic in this topology (Le Breton, 1987). On the other hand, if preferences are continuous and convex and the dimension of the space is suitably bounded then a core does exist (Schofield, 1984).

It occurred to me that the study of voting procedures is at a very advanced state of development. It also occurred to me that such results are largely unintelligible to students or scholars who are not specialists in "social choice theory."

As this book will illustrate, there are several deep, enduring problems that have confronted people who would design rules for the resolution of disputes. Those rules, commonly called constitutions or bylaws, can be found in many entities, including corporations, trade associations, community groups, labor unions, international organizations, and, of course, nation states and other levels of government. Because these entities are in practice parceled out among academic fields—corporations to business and economics, community organizations to sociology and social welfare, nations to political science—the fact they share common analytical problems is sometimes obscured.

The fact is that most areas of social science touch on problems that are dealt with in social choice. Scholars in such diverse areas as corporate finance, local government, parliamentary politics, and international relations can be confronted with questions about multi-person decision-making. In these areas, people try to resolve their differences through voting procedures, or at least we wish they were able to do so. The field of social choice offers many valuable theoretical insights and research strategies that can help us to better understand why decision-making procedures work as they do and how they might be changed for the better.

As is the case in chemistry, physics, or mathematics, one cannot start at the top and expect to understand very much. Instead, a student needs to start by learning the basic terminology, notation, and research strategy, along with the substance of the problem that inspires the research. This book is designed to give the briefest possible treatment of those basic issues. Symbols from logic and mathematics are introduced and explained in the simplest way possible. With the exception of one starred section that can be skipped, a knowledge of calculus or other advanced mathematics is not assumed in this presentation. That doesn't mean I expect this to be an easy read. Rather, the presentation is more or less self-contained. Where possible, interpretations in plain English have been included to highlight the importance of the mathematical findings.

SOCIAL CHOICE: THEORY AND RESEARCH

PAUL E. JOHNSON
University of Kansas

1. WHAT IS SOCIAL CHOICE THEORY?

In newspaper or television coverage of Congress, we are accustomed to hearing reporters discuss "what Congress preferred" or "how Congress decided." Obviously, they would be more precise to say "some of the members of Congress preferred" or "the Majority leader decided," but it does not seem like they are doing much damage. After all, if we think that individual members have rational preferences, it seems like a very small step to believe that Congress as a whole can be treated as if it were a rational entity. It turns out that this supposition is false.

The fact that individual interaction can result in unexpected, possibly nonsensical, social outcomes is a key element in social choice theory. Social choice theory investigates procedures that attempt to "amalgamate" or "blend" the preferences of the many into a social ranking of alternatives. The details of this theory, as it applies to a variety of decision-making situations, are explored in this book. The presentation is aimed to develop a coherent view of the field and its major research problems. Much of the material presented is designed to provide tools and terminology that will enable students to study decision problems on their own. However, there is no gratuitous terminology or mathematics.

The most common starting point for studies of social choice is called the **voter's paradox** (or the paradox of voting). The paradox is the most basic example of how rational individual behavior begets irrational collective decisions. As Black's (1958) excellent history of social choice theory points out, the paradox was recognized at least as early as 1785 by the Marquis de Condorcet. Its implications were not fully understood until the 1950s, when modern-day pioneers of social choice theory, such as Kenneth Arrow and Duncan Black, laid the foundations of the field that this book describes.

1

The Voter's Paradox

Suppose three voters are choosing by majority rule among three brands of pineapple to be served at a fraternity party. For notational purposes, let's refer to the voters by the numbers 1, 2, and 3. The pineapple brands are Dole, Clinton, and Perot. To summarize the voter's preferences, let's use the standard shorthand

Clinton P_1 Perot

to mean that voter 1 (as indicated by the subscript) prefers (as indicated by the P_1) Clinton to Perot. (Think of P_1 as if it were a greater than sign, $>$, so the appeal of Clinton is greater than that of Perot.) When we have many alternatives, we can string them together in the obvious way:

Voter 1: Clinton P_1 Perot P_1 Dole
Voter 2: Dole P_2 Clinton P_2 Perot
Voter 3: Perot P_3 Dole P_3 Clinton

In the grand democratic tradition, the three voters decide to resolve their differences of opinion by majority rule. The elections are to be held pairwise, a series of head-to-head contests between the alternatives. In a contest between the Clinton and Perot brands, Clinton wins with the support of voters 1 and 2. Voter 2 is likely to ask that his favorite, Dole, be considered against Clinton. Dole defeats Clinton with the support of voters 2 and 3. Everything seems settled until Voter 3 observes that his favorite, Perot, defeats Dole with the support of voters 1 and 3. This "voting cycle" is an apparent violation of the principle of **transitivity**. Students might remember the principle of transitivity in elementary mathematics, which states that if $a > b$, and $b > c$, then $a > c$. In the social choice theory, the focus is on preference, symbolized by P, rather than "greater than," but the idea is the same. (There's no subscript on P because it represents the social preference, not an individual's preference.) If majority rule were transitive, we would expect that, if aPb and bPc, then aPc, but in the story of pineapple, transitivity does not hold. Check for yourself by substituting (a = Clinton, b = Perot, and c = Dole).

The voter's paradox presents an example of what we now call a cyclical majority. The term **cyclical majority** was coined by the

Reverend C. L. Dodgson in 1876 to refer to a situation in which no alternative is unbeatable (see Black, 1958). The social decision can jump from one alternative to the next, never settling by majority rule on a single outcome. (Readers might be interested to know that, in addition to studying voting procedures, the Reverend Dodgson also had an interest in fiction. Under the pen name Lewis Caroll, he wrote *Alice in Wonderland.*)

The hallmark of rationality is the ability to rank-order alternatives, to say "I prefer this to that" and "that to the other thing." It is a truly surprising to find that the social preference is incoherent, even when voters are perfectly able to organize their opinions and cast ballots correctly. It is not necessary to introduce mistakes or irrationality on the part of individual participants in order to obtain an incoherent decision. Partly for that reason, social choice models typically do not include such exceptions to rationality in their models. Furthermore, researchers generally believe that irrationality—as evidenced by intransitive preferences—is a rare trait. The first part of the research enterprise is to find a procedure that works when people meet the ideal standard of rationality. After that, the sensitivity of the procedure to changes in the assumptions can be investigated.

The Big Picture

The paradox of voting has motivated the study of voting procedures, but the field of social choice is not defined by the voter's paradox. Social choice theory investigates many kinds of multiperson decision-making problems. The unifying element in social choice studies is the desire to understand "preference aggregation," the way that individual differences combine into a policy that will affect many people. There are other unifying elements, of course. Individual rationality is one of them. Social choice theory, like the field of "rational choice theory" of which it is a part, often begins with a model of individual behavior that emphasizes the pursuit of personal goals. We assume that people have objectives as well as an ability to differentiate and rank the possible outcomes.

If everyone in a group agrees about what ought to be done, there's not much need to worry about how their collective decisions will be made. Any reasonable voting procedure would generate the same outcome. Any individual in the group could be appointed the king and the others would have no reason to worry. That's the beauty of consensus. In reality, people do not always find themselves in total harmony. People disagree about what ought to be done. If a decision benefits some people and harms others, self-interest may motivate a clash of opinions. Selfish people—people who place no weight whatsoever on the happiness of others—will favor decisions that suit them personally. There can be disagreements even among people who are not selfish, of course. Even if all people were interested only in advancing the welfare of the community, they might still disagree about how it ought to be done. As long as people disagree, there is something worth studying.

In social choice theory, as in the broader field of rational choice, individual goals are typically taken as "givens," part of the data provided by a study of a particular situation. This is a practical decision, based in large part on the need to keep research projects manageable. Asking why people like the things they like or why they have a particular political ideology would take us too far from the focal point, which is preference aggregation. That does not mean that the origins of preferences are unimportant or that preferences are somehow permanently fixed, immutable personal traits. It merely means that, barring an exceptional reason to take a different approach, we will take preference information as data for the purposes of building a model. While a decision-making procedure is being administered, it is reasonable to assume that people act as if they are trying to bring about the outcomes they prefer. With few exceptions, the literature has not focused on the possibility that personal goals might change during a short period of time. It should be added that factual evidence about Congress indicates that preferences generally don't change very much (Poole, 1997).

The division between the study of "what is" and "what ought to be" is sometimes blurry in social science. Social choice theory deals with topics that force us to confront questions that are both descriptive and prescriptive in nature. The prescriptive questions—the normative questions—ask us to evaluate a method of voting, to decide whether it is a good way of making a decision. The descriptive questions—the so-called positive questions—are often aimed at finding an underlying structure in our observations. Social choice theories tend to emphasize individualistic behavior, and scholars search in the logic of individual behavior and interaction for explanations of the overall patterns that we think are important. Some might argue that the emphasis on individuality is unrealistic or possibly even cynical.

The normative and positive questions are not entirely distinct. We often need to know how things work in order to make a prescription for change. Suppose we liken a social choice project to a medical examination. The patient is an ailing political system. The paradox of voting is the disease. The descriptive part of the problem deals with the formulation of a model of how individuals interact. We have to suppose, for example, that there are indeed circumstances in which people disagree and need to make a choice. If the model can be analyzed logically—with mathematical tools—then some predictions might be offered about the nature of choices that will emerge. The normative part of the problem deals with the quality of the decision and the procedure being used. If the patient has the disease known as the paradox of voting, as doctors of democratic theory we have a need to comprehend the illness and ascertain its implications. Social choice theory investigates voting procedures the way doctors study anatomy and chemistry: they want to understand why the disease develops and how it can be cured.

One very important philosophical motivation for social choice theory is the general acceptance of the norm of **citizen sovereignty**: the idea that people who live in a society should have a say in public policy (if not directly, then indirectly through representative governmental institutions). The members of a corporate board expect to have input into the decisions that are reached, as do the members of a neighborhood organization. Dictatorship is a bad thing, in other words, and social choice theory is partly aimed at the question of whether the voting-oriented alternatives to dictatorship are workable and fair to the participants. I say "partly" because non-voting-oriented alternatives, such as market exchange, are sometimes introduced as alternative methods of allocating resources. Introducing markets does not change the fundamental fact, however, that the aim is to understand the conditions under which nondictatorial procedures might be feasible.

Framed in that light, some of the most important research questions in social choice are:

- Is there a normatively palatable method of voting that generates a logical (transitive) ordering of alternatives?
- What effects do procedures have on social choices?

- How are people inclined to behave under a given set of conditions?
- What recommendations can we make to people who design political institutions or decision-making procedures?

Research questions like these are usually attacked by a two-step process of model-building and deductive analysis. A **model** is an abstract representation of a situation that is thought to include its most important or essential elements. The abstraction, which is typically phrased with mathematical and logical symbols, allows the deductive analysis. The deductions, which state relationships between variables in the model, are the prize for which the analyst strives. The most important statements that can be supported by such deductions are typically called **theorems**. A **lemma** is a result of less importance that must be proven in the process of establishing a more important theorem. Whether a result is a called a lemma or a theorem is a matter of taste and judgment, rather than rock hard categorization. Leaving the problem of classifying results as theorems or lemmas to posterity, some scholars use the general term **proposition** to refer to the findings that they believe can be supported on the basis of the model.

There are three basic ingredients in a social choice model: a set of alternatives, a list of voters and their preferences, and procedures. Each of these ingredients must be tailored to the substance of the situation being investigated. It seems important to admit at the outset that there are matters of personal judgment and mathematical convenience that shape the modeling enterprise. It is often difficult to separate the essential from the unnecessary details. Of course, this is true in any academic endeavor, and the modeling enterprise has some self-correcting mechanisms. The emphasis on clear, unambiguous assumptions and deductive logic makes it difficult to hide a bogus model. After a research project has completed the preliminary stages of model-building and analysis, one will often be interested in knowing if some assumptions can be "relaxed" or "generalized."

The methods of logic and mathematical analysis play a very big part in social choice theory. Elections seem to lend themselves to a mathematical representation because they typically involve counting and measurement. The assumption that people are purposive actors is naturally modeled as mathematical maximization of an objective function. Beyond building a representation, however, the formal methods are important because they allow the proof (or disproof) of claims about the model. If logical analysis were somehow forbidden, we would be caught in an imponderable and ridiculous series of "is not" and "is too" arguments. The formal analysis lays bare the linkage between the assumptions that create the model and the conclusions that are formed on the basis of it.

An Outline of This Book

In this book, the emphasis is on the mathematical methods and results, rather than the more general democratic theory. The broader philosophical problems of democratic theory and social choice are considered in Riker's *Liberalism against Populism* (1982).

I have divided the theory into two parts: the first focuses on social choice problems in which the set of alternatives is discrete, or categorical, and the second focuses on problems in which the alternatives are continuous. In an election, the set of alternatives might be a simple list of names, such as Dole, Clinton, and Perot. This is an example of a **discrete social choice model**. In a discrete set of alternatives, one typically finds no meaningful ordering among the alternatives. The discrete social choice models have their roots in the earliest of social choice theories, as we shall see. The literature on discrete social choice features Arrow's theorem, a classic statement on the feasibility of designing methods of preference aggregation to meet certain requirements.

On the other hand, if the alternatives can be thought of as an ordered set, represented by points in a continuum, then we have a **spatial model**. The spatial models draws on concepts from geometry, real analysis, and topology to describe the set of alternatives and the tastes of the voters. The spatial model has roots almost as deep and long-standing as the discrete social choice models. Whereas the models of discrete social choice are mathematically simple, the spatial model offers a way to describe a richer, more interesting political world. Studies using the spatial model seem to suit our intuitions about political ideologies, for example. People are not categorized into liberal and conservative. Rather, ideology may range from very liberal to very conservative, and all points in between. If a group is deciding how much money to spend on a project, the alternatives from which they choose are drawn from a continuous space, not a categorical list.

The difference between the discrete and spatial models may be a simple matter of degree. If a discrete model introduces several hundred thousand alternatives, they might reasonably approximate a continuum. Such a model might be rather unmanageable, however. Most theorists would rather use the mathematical tools intended for continuous spaces in such a case, however, and would shift to a spatial model.

In the chapters that follow, then, the analysis proceeds from the discrete social choice model to the spatial model. This is done partly for educational reasons, as classroom experience indicates that the discrete model is more easily grasped and also it sets in place much of the groundwork for the spatial model. Chapter 2 outlines the fundamental rational choice theory as it applies to discrete spaces, and Chapter 3 presents the most influential result, Arrow's theorem. Arrow's theorem poses some questions that motivated the development of the spatial model, which is introduced in Chapter 4. That chapter introduces the mathematical tools that are used to describe preferences when the set of alternatives is a continuum. The unexpected disjuncture between spatial models in which only one continuum is considered and models in which several continua are considered at the same time provokes the separation of the two models in Chapters 5 and 6. The final chapter points out some avenues for future study.

2. FUNDAMENTAL TERMINOLOGY: DISCRETE SOCIAL CHOICE

Undoubtedly the most influential pioneer of modern social choice theory is Nobel Prize winner Kenneth Arrow, whose famous theorem is presented in Chapter 3 of this book. Arrow focused on **discrete** sets of alternatives. The set of alternatives, X, is treated as a list, such as $\{w, x, y, z\}$. The letters w, x, y, and z stand for policies that might be adopted. The society of voters is called N, and each voter has a number: $N = \{1, 2, 3, \ldots, n\}$. [The ellipses ($\ldots$) mean that the reader is supposed to imagine numbers counting up from 3 to any number n.] To refer to any arbitrarily chosen voter in the set, we often use the letter i. In some proofs, we use the letter j to refer to a particular (usually atypical) member of N who is singled out for scrutiny.

Social choice theory uses some terminology and symbols drawn from set theory. Becoming comfortable with these symbols is absolutely vital to success in further study of social choice. The most important symbols are used to represent "membership" of a subset or element in a larger set. In the notation of set theory, we write $W \subseteq X$ to mean that the set W is a **subset** of the set X. The symbol $\subset$ means that W is a **proper subset,** one that includes some, not all, elements from X. The symbol $\in$, meaning "element of," is used to indicate that a particular policy x or y is drawn from X, as in $x \in X$ or $y \in X$, or that a voter named j is part of some coalition S, as in $j \in S$. The symbol $\forall$ means "for all," so $\forall x \in X$ means "for all elements x in the set X." This is useful if we want to say that something is true of all voters: $\forall i \in N$.

Set theory allows us to represent conditional relationships with notation like

$$\{x \in X \mid x \in Z\}$$

This means, speaking literally, "the set of all x from X that are also members of Z." The outer brackets mean "the set of all items meeting these requirements." The vertical bar (or a semicolon) means "such that." This kind of notation is very useful in keeping track of subgroups of voters. For example, we might write

$$\{i \in N \mid x P_i\, y \text{ and } i \in M\}$$

to mean "the set of all individuals from N who prefer x to y and are also members of a set M."

In Arrow's original presentation, the preferences, or tastes, of the voters are represented by weak preference relations. A **weak prefer-**

ence binary relation is customarily denoted by R_i. We write $x R_i y$ to mean that x is as good as or better than y. In contrast to the **strict preference binary relation**, P_i, which was used above, this allows a person to be indifferent between two alternatives. (The term binary means "consisting of two parts"; i.e., alternatives are compared two at a time. All preference relations discussed in this book are binary.) The weak preference relation might be likened to $\geq$, the "greater than or equal to" sign in mathematics. Some of the classic texts in social choice theory (Fishburn, 1973; Sen, 1970) have offered detailed analyses of the logical links between weak and strict preference relations.

The main reason for using the weak preference relation is that it takes indifference into account. No information is lost by taking R_i, instead of P_i, as the starting point for analysis. If $x R_i y$ and it is not true that $(y R_i x)$, then it must be that $x P_i y$. However, if $x R_i y$ and $y R_i x$, then it must be that voter i is indifferent. The notation $x I_i y$ means that i is indifferent between x and y. Because R_i includes indifference, it is meaningful to write $x R_i x$: x is as good as itself. Because of this fact, R_i is a **complete binary relation**, meaning that, given any two alternatives, $x, y \in X$, either $x R_i y$ or $y R_i x$ or both. A strict preference relation is not complete because it does not allow x to be preferred to itself, so $x P_i x$ is not allowed.

As a mathematical aside, I should warn readers that it is increasingly common in the academic literature for the weak preference relation to be introduced as $R \subseteq X \times X$. The comparison of two alternatives, x and y, is represented as the ordered pair, such as (x, y) to indicate $x R y$. If x is as good as y, we write $(x, y) \in R$. This is bewildering at first, but it is just notation. The preference relation, R, is thought of as a set containing ordered pairs. What is the nature of this list of pairs? First, consider the term $X \times X$, which is the **Cartesian product** of X with itself. A Cartesian product of any two sets, say W and Z, is the list of all pairs that can be formed by picking one item from W and one from Z. Using set notation,

$$W \times Z = \{(w, z) \mid w \in W \text{ and } z \in Z\}$$

That means $W \times Z$ includes all the ordered pairs that can be created by taking one element from X for the first coordinate and an element from Z for the second. If $X = \{x, y, z\}$, then the Cartesian product $X \times X$ has nine points: $X \times X = \{(x, x), (x, y), (x, z), (y, x),$

$(y, y), (y, z), (z, x), (z, y), (z, z)$}. Next, consider the weak preference relation R is a subset of $X \times X$. For example, $R =$ {$(x, y), (y, z),$ $(x, z), (x, x), (y, y), (z, z)$}. Alternative x is as good as y, y is as good as z, and x is as good as z. Hence, R is transitive! In addition, R is complete, since $(x, x) \in R$, $(y, y) \in R$, and $(z, z) \in R$. It makes little difference whether we use the older notation and think about R as a weak ordering on X or more technically as a subset of $X \times X$. Writing xRy is the same as $(x, y) \in R$. The newer notation is a bit more elegant, mathematically speaking, and it emphasizes the fact that a binary relation is a collection of ordered pairs.

3. ARROW'S THEOREM

Arrow's theorem, first published in 1951, is the starting point for modern social choice theory. His research was motivated by the then-current research questions of welfare economics. At that time, a substantial number of scholars had been attempting to develop indices of social welfare that could be used in policy formulation. Imagine how pleasant policy-making would be if there were a formula for calculating the socially optimal result! One need only tally together the interests of the people in a society to find out what is good for them. Such a social welfare function, whether it is based on a voting process or some other means, would be truly useful. The selfish claims of various interest groups could be deflected—with good justification—by policy-makers who employ the function. Arrow (1951) called his theorem a possibility theorem because it shed light on the possibility of developing such a social welfare function. Without letting the cat out of the bag, one might note that many authors have since called it Arrow's impossibility theorem.

The Social Preference Function

The first step is to define three new terms, $\mathscr{R}$, $\mathscr{R}^n$, and R^n. Let $\mathscr{R}$ be the set of all possible weak preference relations on X. This includes all possible orderings of the alternatives. Each voter has preferences drawn from $\mathscr{R}$, so $R_i \in \mathscr{R} \; \forall i \in N$. A **social preference profile** R^n is a collection of individual preference relations, one for each voter $R^n = (R_1, R_2, \ldots, R_n)$. To beat the notation into the ground, it is plain that $R^n \in \mathscr{R}^n$. That is, any particular social preference profile R^n is an element of $\mathscr{R}^n = \mathscr{R} \times \mathscr{R} \times \cdots \times \mathscr{R}$ (the n-times Cartesian product of $\mathscr{R}$).

Arrow discussed a social welfare function (SWF), a way of combining the opinions of the members of a society into an index of social welfare. Because that term confused some readers and carried emotional baggage for others, it is now better to call it a **social preference function**, a function that gives back a social preference relation, an element $R \in \mathscr{R}$, for each possible preference profile, $R^n \in \mathscr{R}^n$. Formally, a social preference function is specified $F: \mathscr{R}^n \to \mathscr{R}$. [This is standard mathematical notation for functions. Readers might have seen $f: X \to Y$. The function f takes any element in a set X and gives back an element from Y. We might write $y = f(x)$ to refer to the fact that if we are given a particular element $x \in X$, we are given back a particular element $y \in Y$. X is called the **domain**, which f *maps* into Y, the **range**.]

If there were an acceptable social preference function, $F: \mathcal{R}^n \to \mathcal{R}$, then given a preference profile R^n, one could choose on behalf of a society by consulting R, the social preference relation. Since R is complete and transitive, the society would have no difficulty choosing optimal social policy. The optimal policy—the social choice—would be the maximal element:

$$\{x \in X \mid xRy \text{ for all } y \in X\}$$

In many instances, it is convenient to refer to this construction as the social choice rule. In addition, since the social preference relation R is complete and transitive, social indifference, I, and a strict social preference relation, P, can be derived in the obvious way.

The social preference relation R is a binary relation, meaning that it can tell us whether one proposal is better than another. Often, we assume that this binary relation is produced by a procedure that compares two alternatives at a time in some kind of voting procedure. This does not mean, however, that Arrow's theorem applies only to binary voting procedures. R is a binary relation, but it may be produced by nonbinary voting procedures. Any procedure that produces a ranking of five candidates—such as a measurement of their heights or intelligence quotients—can be represented by a complete and transitive binary relation. For example, consider diving contests in which divers are awarded scores by several judges and in the end the contestants are ranked by the sum of their scores across several dives. The binary social preference relation R can be calculated by comparing the scores earned by any two alternatives, i.e., diver x finished as well or better than diver y if the point total of x is as high or higher than y.

Arrow's Possibility Theorem

The sad fact, as we shall see, is that there is no social preference function (sometimes will say social choice procedure to break up the monotony) that meets some apparently minimal (and seemingly easy-to-meet) criteria of democratic decision-making. In what follows, F is the social preference function, a rule that translates the preferences of individuals into a social ranking of alternatives. The plan is to develop a list of requirements for F that seem, at least on the surface, to be unobjectionable, and then prove logically that they are impossible to satisfy.

The modern version of Arrow's theorem deals with four properties of social choice, which are known (for short) as universal domain, Pareto principle, independence from irrelevant alternatives, and nondictatorship. We will define and consider each in turn.

> **U: Universal Domain.** For each possible social preference profile R^n, the social preference function prescribes a weak social preference relation. More succinctly, $F: \mathscr{R}^n \to \mathscr{R}$.

Comment. This assumption is typically called universal domain, but it would perhaps be better to call it universal domain–rational range. It has two significant parts because the function must have a specified domain and range. In this presentation, the requirement that the domain must be equal to $\mathscr{R}^n$ will be referred to as Ua, and the restriction that the range must be $\mathscr{R}$ is called Ub. Since the property U can be violated either by limiting the domain or exceeding the range requirement, it is useful to separate these requirements as Ua and Ub.

Property Ua is quite straightforward. It is unacceptable, from a democratic standpoint, to declare that people cannot vote because of their opinions. All that we can insist is that the voters be rational—have preference orderings drawn from $\mathscr{R}$. Hence, all profiles drawn from the set $\mathscr{R}^n$ must be admissible.

Property Ub is a very important part of the theorem. It requires that the range of the social preference function be limited to the weak preference orderings. The social preference function must give output drawn from $\mathscr{R}$, meaning it must result in a complete and transitive weak preference relation. If a result of applying a social preference function is not in this set, then social decision-making is somehow irrational, either incomplete or intransitive.

> **P: Pareto Efficiency.** If $x P_i y$ for all $i \in N$, then $x P y$.

Comment. When everyone in society strictly prefers one policy to another, it would be a perverse world indeed if the unanimously preferred alternative were not socially preferred.

> **ND: Nondictatorship:** There is no dictator, a person j such that $x P_j y$ implies $x P y$.

Comment. It is important to remember that j gets his/her way, regardless of what the other members of the society prefer. No sane proponent of democratic procedures would knowingly advocate a system in which one person is able to decide policy for the whole of society without regard for the preferences of the others.

IIA: Independence from Irrelevant Alternatives. The social preference relation between x and y is unaffected by changes in the position of an irrelevant alternative, z, in the preference profile.

Consider two preference profiles, $R^n \in \mathcal{R}^n$ and $Q^n \in \mathcal{R}^n$, and suppose the social preference function indicates a social preference relation R when the preference profile is R^n and it selects Q when the profile is Q^n. IIA requires that if voter preferences, R^n and Q^n, agree on the subset $\{x, y\}$ meaning $x R_i y$ if and only if $x Q_i y$ for all i, then the social preference ought to be the same: $x R y$ if and only if $x Q y$.

Comment. This one is a bit more complicated than the other properties and has been the most frequent source of confusion. To illustrate, consider IIA as it might apply to you as an individual. You are deciding from a dinner menu. On the menu there is fish, chicken, and beef. The waiter says, "between beef and chicken, which do you prefer?" IIA requires that your choice between beef and chicken should be the same, no matter whether you rank fish as the best, the worst, in between, or indifferent. It is an irrelevant alternative in the sense that, when you are comparing beef and chicken, fish is not in the set from which you are choosing. The word "irrelevant" does not have a pejorative connotation. It simply refers to the alternatives that are left out of the set from which you are asked to choose.

IIA has roughly the same meaning in a social choice problem. In Figure 3.1, consider a choice between banquet menu items, beef, chicken, and fish, by three voters, colorfully named 1, 2, and 3. Note only the position of fish changes from profile to profile. Property IIA says the social choice between beef and chicken should be the same in each of the four preference profiles. More formally, you can take any two profiles from 1 through 4 (or the other profiles you could create by moving fish around) and call one of them $R^3 = (R_1, R_2, R_3)$ and the other one $Q^3 = (Q_1, Q_2, Q_3)$. Let the social choice rule specify that when the voter preferences are R^3, then the social preference relation is R, and for Q^3, the social preference relation is Q. Property IIA requires {beef R chicken} if and only if {beef Q chicken}, and {chicken R beef} if and only if {chicken Q beef}.

Arrow's Theorem (The General Possibility Theorem). If there are three or more alternatives in X, there is no social preference function that satisfies U, P, IIA, and ND.

Proof of Arrow's Theorem. The proof of Arrow's theorem is worth going through because it illustrates the power of the formal represen-

Profile 1

Voter 1	*Voter 2*	*Voter 3*
beef	chicken	chicken
chicken	beef	beef
fish	fish	fish

Profile 2

Voter 1	*Voter 2*	*Voter 3*
fish	fish	fish
beef	chicken	chicken
chicken	beef	beef

Profile 3

Voter 1	*Voter 2*	*Voter 3*
beef	chicken	fish
fish	fish	chicken
chicken	beef	beef

Profile 4

Voter 1	*Voter 2*	*Voter 3*
beef	chicken	chicken
chicken	fish	beef
fish	beef	fish

Figure 3.1. Illustration of Independence from Irrelevant Alternatives: The Social Preference Relation between Beef and Chicken Should Be the Same for Each of the Four Profiles. The Voters' Ranking of the Alternatives Is Indicated from Top (Most Desirable) to Bottom (Least Desirable)

tation. This is a standard method of proof, one that was first enunciated by Arrow and has been refined many times (see Arrow, 1963, pp. 97–100; Blau, 1972; Kreps, 1990, pp. 178–180). It is quite an elegant and efficient proof. It shows clearly the importance of each condition, providing evidence for the parsimony of Arrow's setup. The strategy of proof is to show that a complete and transitive social preference relation, R, that satisfies U, P, and IIA, must violate ND.

Since dictatorship is a property of strict preference, to make our life easier from this point on, we will consider only strict preference relations, P_i. In restricting attention to P_i, we are ruling out the possibility of individual indifference. This does not reduce the power of the proof. According to property U, the social choice rule should apply to all possible social preference profiles, including strict preference profiles. By doing so, we show not only that P, IIA, and ND are inconsistent with U, but also that P, IIA, and ND are inconsistent with a more restrictive version of U that admits only strict preferences. (If P, IIA, and ND are inconsistent with admissability of all strict preference relations, they are surely inconsistent with admissability of weak preference relations.) Hence, if you suspected that some kind of trick with transitive indifference was at work, you were wrong.

The proof begins with a definition: A coalition M is *decisive for x against y* if $x P_i y$ for all $i \in M$ and $y P_i x$ for all $i \in N - M$ imply $x P y$. (The subset M is decisive if it gets its way when it is opposed by all nonmembers.) Note the Pareto property guarantees that N is decisive—if everyone prefers x to y, x is socially preferred to y.

Let D be the set of coalitions that are decisive for some pair and let V be a "smallest coalition in D," a coalition that $|V| \le |M|$ for all $M \in D$.

Claim 1. There is some pair of alternatives x and y for which a single person j is decisive (for brevity, we might write $|V| = 1$ to indicate that the smallest coalition in D is a single person).

This is proven by finding a contradiction that flows from the hypothesis $|V| > 1$. Let j be a single member of V, let $U = V - \{j\}$, and let $W = N - V$. If V is decisive for x against y, it must mean that member j and all members of U prefer x to y and the members of W are opposed. Because of independence of irrelevant alternatives, we can insert the third alternative z anywhere into the preference orderings of the voters and the decisiveness of V over x and y continues to hold. Hence, the preference profile could be

preferences of j: $x P_j y P_j z$
preferences of $k \in U$: $z P_k x P_k y$
preferences of $k \in W$: $y P_k z P_k x$

Recall that $x P_j y P_j z$ means that $x P_j y$, $y P_j z$ and, by transitivity, $x P_j z$.

Given this profile of preferences, x will be preferred to z, meaning that j is decisive. To justify that conclusion, follow these steps (and their explanations on the right):

1. $x P y$ We assumed V is decisive for x against y.
2. $y P z$ Use this trick: since only members of U prefer z to y, and U is not a decisive coalition, it cannot be that $z R y$. Hence, it must be that $y P z$.
3. $x P z$ Because P is transitive (according to condition Ub), 1 and 2 imply 3.

The only voter who preferred x to z was j, so j is decisive for x against z! Hence, V could not have been the smallest coalition in D because a single member, j, is decisive for x against z. That is the contradiction we wanted, so now we know $|V| = 1$.

Now wipe the slate clean. The next chore is to show that individual decisiveness between any pair of alternatives implies a more general dictatorship. The proof is methodical, showing clearly the importance of properties P and IIA.

Claim 2. If member j is decisive for x against y, then j is a dictator. This is proven by showing that whenever j prefers one alternative to another, then the society does too. We have to show this for four different possible pairings of the alternatives, (z, y), (z, x), (x, w), and (z, w).

Claim 2a. For any $z \in X$, if member j is decisive for x against y, then $z P_j y \rightarrow z P y$. To avoid triviality, assume z is not the same alternative as x (i.e., $z \neq x$).

Because of IIA, we can place z anywhere we want in the preferences of voter j and the rest of the voters $W = N - \{j\}$ and still preserve j's decisiveness over x and y:

preferences of j: $z P_j x P_j y$
preferences for every voter $k \in W$: $y P_k x$ and $z P_k x$ (note we don't set z vs y)

From this preference information, observe

4. $z P x$ By the Pareto property, since $z P_i x \; \forall i \in N$.
5. $x P y$ Recall j is decisive for x against y.
6. $z P y$ Because P is transitive.

Note we assumed only that member j ranked z over y. We assumed nothing about the preferences of W between z and y. Since no matter how W ranks z and y, $z P_j y$ implies $z P y$, so j is a dictator over the pair (z, y).

Claim 2b. For any $z \in X$, if member j is decisive for x against y, then $z P_j x \rightarrow z P x$. Again to avoid triviality, $z \neq y$. Because of property U, the social choice rule must be applicable to this preference information:

preferences of j: $z P_j y P_j x$
preferences of $k \in W$: $y P_k x$ and $y P_k z$ (note we don't set x vs z)

Reasoning from this, observe

7. $z P y$ Recall from step 6 that j is decisive for z against y. This holds here because of IIA—the relative ranking of z and y is unchanged from Claim 2a. Only the ranking of x, an alternative irrelevant to the comparison of z and y, changed.
8. $y P x$ By the Pareto property, since y is preferred to x unanimously.
9. $z P x$ Because P is transitive, 7 and 8 imply 9.

Member j is thus a dictator over the pair (z, x).

Claim 2c. For any $w \in X$, if member j is decisive for x against y, $x P_j w \rightarrow x P w$. Because of property U, we can apply the social preference function to these preferences:

preferences of j: $x P_j y P_j w$
preferences of $k \in W$: $y P_k w$ and $y P_k x$

10. $x P y$ Voter j is decisive, by assumption.
11. $y P w$ Pareto property.
12. $x P w$ P is transitive.

Member j is the dictator over the pair (x, w)

Claim 2d. For any $z, w \in X$, if j is decisive for x against y, $z P_j w \rightarrow z P w$. This is the big result. If j is decisive for any pair x, y, j is a dictator for any other pair z, w. For the nontrivial case in which neither z or w is the same as x or y, consider these preferences for j:

preferences of j: $z P_j x P_j w$

We are free to insert x between z and w because doing so does not affect the relative ranking of z and w (application of IIA, again):

13. $z P x$ Step 9 above.
14. $x P w$ Step 12 above.
15. $z P w$ Transitivity.

Member j is the dictator over the pair (z, w). No matter what the other members of society feel about z and w, j's favorite is adopted. That's the definition of dictatorship, of course, so the proof is complete. (In journals, proofs typically end with the acronym QED, which stands for the Latin *quod erat demonstrandum*, meaning "that which was to have been demonstrated." In jest, it is often pronounced as "quite enough done.")

The Meaning of Arrow's Theorem

To risk pointing out the obvious, Arrow's theorem has tremendous implications for modern democratic theory. In the ideal world, we would like to have a social choice procedure that can take into account the diversity of opinion in society and give back a social preference ordering. This social preference ordering indicates, for any w and z, that wRz, zRw, or both. We want the social preference ordering to be complete and transitive. Transitivity is a hallmark of coherent and rational judgment. The social choice procedure should satisfy other desirable normative democratic properties as well. It should not make one person a dictator (property ND). It should work no matter what are the opinions of the voters (property U). It is hard to quibble with the Pareto principle that unanimous preference for x over y should imply a social preference xPy. The IIA property—on first glance at least—seems just as reasonable. IIA says that the social ranking of x and y should be identical when the social choice rule is applied to each of two profiles that contain identical preferences concerning x and y among all voters.

Many students have complained that the theorem is imponderable. To cut through the fog of abstraction, it is important to work through its implications from a variety of perspectives. Perhaps at least one of these implications will hit home.

Implication 1. To solve the problem of intransitive social preference, one might be forced to disallow some voter profiles. In other words, sometimes people will have to be disenfranchised.

To this point, the social preference function has been treated in an abstract way. It might be an ordering built up by the application of any method of voting or, in fact, any method of ranking alternatives. The meaning of the theorem can be brought more into the open if we focus on a particular method of voting—majority rule. Majority rule is a widely used method of group decision-making. Informally, majority rule states that the winning alternative is the one with the support of more than one-half of the voters. More formally, consider this definition. If a person prefers x to y, $xP_i y$, then that person votes for x over y. Indifferent people abstain, so x beats y if more people with a preference prefer x to y, or

$$xPy \quad \text{if } |\{i \in N : xP_i\, y\}| > |\{i \in N : yP_i\, x\}|$$

The outer brackets, which look like "absolute value" signs, indicate cardinality, the number of items in a set. Inside this expression, the semicolon means "such that." This is used here, instead of the more standard vertical bar, because there is danger of confusion resulting from the usage of the vertical bar in another part of the expression. Hence, $|\{i \in N : xP_i\, y\}|$ would read literally as "the number of voters in N who prefer x to y."

Here the focus is on the violation of condition Ua, a violation that we commit in order to find a procedure that satisfies all of the other conditions. Majority rule is such a procedure. It satisfies ND, P, and IIA, and if we assume it satisfies Ub, it must mean we violate Ua. Majority rule is an important starting place in voting theory, not only because it has been used for centuries, but also because, according to May's (1952) theorem, majority rule is the only method of choosing between two alternatives that meets the normative requirements of strong monotonicity, duality, and anonymity. Strong monotonicity means that if there is tie vote, then a change in one voter's preference from $yP_i\, x$ to $xP_i\, y$ will cause x to win. Duality (sometimes called neutrality) requires that if we reverse everyone's preference, so $xP_i\, y$ becomes $yP_i\, x$ and $yP_i\, x$ becomes $xP_i\, y$, then the social choice is reversed. Anonymity (sometimes called undifferentiated-ness) demands that if the index numbering the voters is shuffled, the social choice is unchanged. Since majority rule has this strong justification when there are only two alternatives, it is natural to investigate whether its appeal stretches when alternatives are added. The enduring problem is that majority rule's attraction does not extend to situations involving three or more alternatives.

How badly do we need to restrict the domain of the social preference function in order to eliminate cycles? To provide some insight into this problem, let's work out the details behind the voter's paradox. Considering strict preference orderings only, when $|X| = 3$ and $N = 3$, how many ways are there to create preference profiles? There are six ways to order x, y, and z. With three voters, when each one might have one of six possible preference orderings, there are $6^3 = 216$ possible preference profiles.

(A mathematical aside on counting. There are $6 = 3! = 3 \cdot 2 \cdot 1$ ways to sort three alternatives into ordered triplets. The motivation for the formula $3 \cdot 2 \cdot 1$ goes like this. You start with a free choice of any of the three elements to take the top position in the preference order—that's the 3. To fill in the second element, you can take either of two remaining alternatives—that's the 2. On the last you have only one remaining to pick—that's the 1. In general, the number of ways to order N things is $N!$ There is an easy way to know that there are 6^3 preference profiles. In functional analysis, to represent the set of all functions from a set X into a set Y, mathematicians write Y^X. If X and Y are discrete sets, Y^X is simply the set of all ways to map the elements of X into Y, and, for discrete sets, it happens to be that the number of functions from X to Y equals the real number $|Y|^{|X|}$. That is how we know that the number of ways to map three people into each of six preference profiles is 6^3. If you take a group of 10 people and have to assign each person to either of two groups, how many ways are there? 2^{10}. If you have 22 people and 19 possible preference orderings, how many profiles can be created? 19^{22}. In a set with N elements, 2^N is often called the **power set** because it represents all subsets on N, including N itself and the empty set $\varnothing$.)

In Figure 3.2, one can study the 36 possible preference orderings in which voter 1's preferences are $x P_1 y P_1 z$. (Readers who have a lot of free time might consider creating the 180 other possible preference profiles.) If one checks each of the 36 profiles to see if the majority rule generates a transitive ordering, the result is not as bleak as one might have thought. Only two of 36 profiles lead to a majority rule voting cycle. The profiles that cause cycles are numbered 23 and 28 (shown boxed).

It is debatable whether or not, in the "real world," the 2 of 36 preference profiles would actually arise. It is not obvious that we should assume the preference orderings in reality are randomly assigned, so it might be dangerous to claim that the probability of a cycle with three voters and three alternatives is $2/36 \approx 0.056$. Nevertheless, the approach is suggestive. If preferences are assumed to be strict, then only 5.6% of the time will we be forced to cancel the election for fear of intransitivity. That will seem like a high percentage to some readers and a low percentage to others.

When there are three alternatives, a majority rule cycle must necessarily "go through" all three alternatives. If the number of

	1			2			3			4			5			6		
P_1:	x	y	z	x	y	z	x	y	z	x	y	z	x	y	z	x	y	z
P_2:	x	y	z	x	y	z	x	y	z	x	y	z	x	y	z	x	y	z
P_3:	x	y	z	x	z	y	y	x	z	y	z	x	z	x	y	z	y	x

	7			8			9			10			11			12		
P_1:	x	y	z	x	y	z	x	y	z	x	y	z	x	y	z	x	y	z
P_2:	x	z	y	x	z	y	x	z	y	x	z	y	x	z	y	x	z	y
P_3:	x	y	z	x	z	y	y	x	z	y	z	x	z	x	y	z	y	x

	13			14			15			16			17			18		
P_1:	x	y	z	x	y	z	x	y	z	x	y	z	x	y	z	x	y	z
P_2:	y	x	z	y	x	z	y	x	z	y	x	z	y	x	z	y	x	z
P_3:	x	y	z	x	z	y	y	x	z	y	z	x	z	x	y	z	y	x

	19			20			21			22			23			24		
P_1:	x	y	z	x	y	z	x	y	z	x	y	z	x	y	z	x	y	z
P_2:	y	z	x	y	z	x	y	z	x	y	z	x	y	z	x	y	z	x
P_3:	x	y	z	x	z	y	y	x	z	y	z	x	z	x	y	z	y	x

	25			26			27			28			29			30		
P_1:	x	y	z	x	y	z	x	y	z	x	y	z	x	y	z	x	y	z
P_2:	z	x	y	z	x	y	z	x	y	z	x	y	z	x	y	z	x	y
P_3:	x	y	z	x	z	y	y	x	z	y	z	x	z	x	y	z	y	x

	31			32			33			34			35			36		
P_1:	x	y	z	x	y	z	x	y	z	x	y	z	x	y	z	x	y	z
P_2:	z	y	x	z	y	x	z	y	x	z	y	x	z	y	x	z	y	x
P_3:	x	y	z	x	z	y	y	x	z	y	z	x	z	x	y	z	y	x

Figure 3.2. The 36 Profiles in which $x P_1 y \; y P_1 z$: For Simplicity, This Is Represented $x \; y \; z$

alternatives is larger, it may be that a cycle in the social preference ordering is not "global," in the sense that some alternatives are not in the cycle. This is the focus of the next implication.

Implication 2. Some violations of Ub are not necessarily harmful.

Whether or not an intransitivity can be tolerated depends on whether the voters are able to find meaning in, or at least some use for, the results of their decision process. There's no way to argue that a global cycle—a cycle through all alternatives—generates a meaningful social ordering. Other violations might not seem so bad.

Does Arrow's theorem mean that there will always be global voting cycles? Absolutely not. When there are more than three alternatives, there is a difference between "cyclical majorities" and "intransitivities." For example, a social preference ordering of the following kind is intransitive, but there is an unbeatable alternative:

$$w P x, w P y, w P z, x P y, y P z, z P x$$

The existence of an unbeatable alternative means there is no global cycle in this case. The intransitivity is a local cycle involving only x, y, and z.

To explore this kind of situation, we introduce the concept of a Condorcet winner. A **Condorcet winner** is an alternative that can defeat each of the other alternatives in a pairwise majority vote. Condorcet recommended that if one alternative wins a majority when paired against each of the other alternatives, then it should be the social choice. The social preference relation need not be transitive for a Condorcet winner to exist.

Example. Under majority rule with four alternatives $\{w, x, y, z\}$, it may be that w is a Condorcet winner but also that there is a cycle involving x, y, and z. Consider these transitive preferences for three voters:

Voter 1: $w P_1 x P_1 y P_1 z$
Voter 2: $w P_2 y P_2 z P_2 x$
Voter 3: $w P_3 z P_3 x P_3 y$

Obviously, w defeats x, y, and z in a series of head-on comparisons, so w is a Condorcet winner. However, there is an intransitivity in the social preference ordering: $x P y$, $y P z$, $z P x$. Many would argue that this is not such a worrisome situation because the intransitivity is confined to the bottom of the social preference ordering. This possibility sheds some light on the significance of Arrow's theorem. The theorem does not say "global cycles are always possible." The intransitivity in the social ordering might not be a compelling problem.

How often is the intransitivity of this benign sort? When there are three voters and three alternatives, the probability of a randomly chosen profile having no Condorcet winner is 0.056. There are studies that have calculated the probability that no Condorcet winner will exist as the numbers of voters and alternatives are increased. Results, illustrated in Table 3.1, indicate that the probability that there will be no Condorcet winner increases as the electorate and alternative set is expanded. With eight alternatives and five voters, there will be no Condorcet winner in about one-third of all randomly drawn strict preference profiles.

These calculations are done with profiles built from strict preference relations only. What if some voters are allowed to be indifferent? This significantly increases the number of profiles that must be inspected, of course. In addition to voters with preferences such as $x P_i y P_i z$, we have $x I_i y I_i z$, $x P_i y I_i z$, $x I_i y P_i z$, $y P_i z I_i x$, $y I_i z P_i x$, and $z P_i x I_i y$. If all of these preference relations are equally likely, what then? Results of a computer simulation analysis reported by Jones, Radcliff, Taber, and Timpone (1995) add food for thought. With three voters, randomly chosen from this larger list, the probability that there will be no majority winner is a staggering 0.333. (If one voter is indifferent and the others are opposed, the election is a tie, and so there is no winner.) As alternatives are added, the probability that there will be no majority rule winner rises. However,

TABLE 3.1
The Probability of Cycles

Number of Alternatives	Number of Voters							
	3	5	7	9	11	25	49	Infinity
3	0.056	0.069	0.075	0.078	0.080	0.084	0.086	0.088
4	0.111	0.139	0.150	0.156	0.160	0.169	0.172	0.176
5	0.160	0.200	0.215	0.224	0.229	0.242	0.246	0.251
6	0.202	0.251	0.271	0.281	0.228	0.303	0.309	0.315
7	0.239	0.296	0.318					0.369
8	0.271	0.334	0.359					0.415
49								0.841

NOTES: What are the chances that there will NOT be a Condorcet winner when voter preferences are drawn randomly from the set of all strict preference relations? These calculations are offered in Ordeshook (1986, p. 58). Blank spaces indicate the calculations were not done because they were computationally prohibitive (demanded too much computer time).

in contrast to the strict preference case, adding voters causes the probability to decline. For example, if there are 501 voters, with six alternatives, the probability that there will be no Condorcet winner is 0.286.

Even if there is no Condorcet winner, implying there is a problem of cyclical majorities, there may not be a global cycle, one that includes all of the alternatives. Consider this example.

Example. Add alternatives u and v to the previous preference profile:

Voter 1: $u P_1 v P_1 w P_1 x P_1 y P_1 z$
Voter 2: $v P_2 w P_2 u P_2 y P_2 z P_2 x$
Voter 3: $w P_3 u P_3 v P_3 z P_3 x P_3 y$

There is a majority rule cycle at the top of the social preference relation, $u P v$, $v P w$, and $w P u$. There is also cycle at the bottom, $x P y$, $y P z$, and $z P x$. However, the two cycles do not "overlap." Any of the top three elements, u, v, and w, can defeat each of the bottom three. In this example, the u, v, and w are a **top-cycle set**. The idea of a top-cycle set was proposed because it was believed that a set of desirable alternatives could be singled out at the top of the social preference relation. Since any element in the top cycle set can defeat any of lower alternatives, there is no way for majority rule to "wander out" of the top cycle. If the top-cycle set is small, then the voting cycles could be confined to a small set of relatively desirable policies. The top-cycle set is formally defined as

$$X^{\text{top}} = \left\{ x \in X \mid \text{there is no } y \in X - X^{\text{top}} \text{ such that } y P x \right\}$$

(Here $X - X^{\text{top}}$ is the complement of X^{top}, the set of points in X that are not in X^{top}.) In the first example, $X^{\text{top}} = \{w\}$, the Condorcet winner w. In the second, $X^{\text{top}} = \{u, v, w\}$. If there is a small top-cycle set, one might argue that intransitivities in the social preference relation are not a significant problem. One might suspect that Arrow's possibility theorem does not present such a formidable challenge to democratic theory (the classic statement of this view is Tullock, 1967).

Before you conclude that a big dent has been smashed into the general possibility theorem, however, you will have to consider the evidence from the multidimensional spatial model of voting that is considered later in this book. The multidimensional model leads to a highly surprising result: when there is an infinite number of alternatives, the top-cycle set is likely to include all of the alternatives.

Implication 3. Otherwise unobjectionable methods—ones that lead to transitive social preference relations—often do so by introducing "intensity" of preference and therefore violate IIA.

It is often believed that one can make a more meaningful decision by being quantitative. Each voter might be asked to rank each alternative on a scale from 1 to 10, and then the winner might be the sum of the scores. Methods like that, known as "scoring" methods, generate a transitive ordering. They are not going to violate the Pareto principle or the nondictatorship requirement, so it must be they violate independence from irrelevant alternatives. How so?

Consider the voting method known as the Borda count. This is a well known scoring method of voting, named in honor of Jean-Charles de Borda, an early (1781) proponent. Each voter orders the alternatives from most to least desirable and then assigns points (0 for the least desirable, 1 for the second-worst, on up to $m - 1$ points for the most desirable). The points are added and the alternative with the most points wins. This procedure violates the principle of IIA.

To be specific, suppose there are four alternatives, w, x, y, and z. The voters rank these alternatives as follows, from most to least desirable:

Voter 1: $w P_1 x P_1 y P_1 z$
Voter 2: $w P_2 x P_2 z P_2 y$
Voter 3: $z P_3 y P_3 w P_3 x$
Voter 4: $x P_4 z P_4 w P_4 y$
Voter 5: $x P_5 y P_5 w P_5 z$

The rankings indicate, for example, that I would assign three points to w, two to x, one to y, and zero to z. Adding the points assigned by the voters, the totals are $w = 9$, $x = 10$, $z = 6$, and $y = 5$. Hence, the social preference ordering is

$$x P w P z P y$$

This is obviously a transitive social preference ordering. From this ordering, we can state unequivocally that $x P w$. A little fiddling will convince you that the Borda procedure provides a complete and transitive social ordering for all profiles that you can design. Hence, property U is satisfied. Since the Borda count provides such an ordering, we know it must violate one of the other properties of Arrow's theorem. Conditions P and ND are obviously satisfied, so IIA must be violated.

To illustrate the violation of IIA, take the preferences and make a few changes in the positioning of the "irrelevant" alternatives y and z. This is done without changing the relative placement of x and w in any of the voters' rankings:

Voter 1: $w P_1 x P_1 y P_1 z$
Voter 2: $w P_2 x P_2 z P_2 y$
Voter 3: $z P_3 w P_3 y P_3 x$
Voter 4: $x P_4 w P_4 z P_4 y$
Voter 5: $x P_5 y P_5 w P_5 z$

According to the Borda count, the totals are $w = 11$, $x = 10$, $z = 5$, and $y = 4$. The social preference ordering is thus

$$w P x P z P y$$

On the basis of this, we would say that $w P x$. Note the social preference between x and w has been reversed, from $x P w$ to $w P x$, even though the voters opinions about the relative desirability of w and x were not changed. (The reader can verify that in both sets of preferences, $w P_1 x$, $w P_2 x$, $w P_3 x$, $x P_4 w$, and $x P_5 w$.) This is the kind of thing that the IIA property is supposed to rule out.

There are other quirks that arise with the use of the Borda method (see Riker, 1982), but we emphasize only one additional point. This problem was noted by Condorcet in his early criticism of Borda's method. In the first example, we found that the Borda winner was x. Note, however, that if a majority election is held pitting w against x, w wins, 3 to 2. In fact, w is a Condorcet winner—it defeats each of the other alternatives in a head-on contest—and yet the Borda procedure does not choose it. This weakness of the Borda procedure seems quite serious, at least if you believe that the Condorcet winner should be chosen.

These are not the only implications that might be derived from Arrow's theorem. There are hundreds of articles in the journals that probe various modifications of the theorem. Kelly's (1978) book, *Arrow Impossibility Theorems*, offers a comprehensive tour. The reader is left with the impression that the fundamental contradiction between IIA, U, ND, and P cannot be dissolved. A minor weakening of one requirement might solve the contradiction, but in turn a slight change in the other conditions will make the contradiction reappear. It now is clear that the theorem is not based on a trivial combination of unusual requirements. Instead, it leads strongly to the conclusion that the basic conditions that we wish we could have in a method of democratic decision-making are not compatible with each other. As William Riker was fond of saying, Arrow's theorem means that procedures can be fair, or logical, but not always both.

4. FUNDAMENTAL TERMINOLOGY: CONTINUOUS SETS OF ALTERNATIVES

Suppose a group is considering two alternatives, x and y. One member of the group says, "I've got it. Lets average them. I propose $\frac{1}{2}x + \frac{1}{2}y$." With discrete sets of alternatives, that's a crazy proposal. If the alternatives are drawn from a continuum, it might not be crazy. Generally speaking, a **spatial model** is a model in which the alternatives are drawn from a mathematically structured space. Most often, the alternatives are thought to have the properties of real numbers, which means they can be multiplied by constants and added or subtracted from one another. Such models are the topic of the next three chapters.

The Euclidean Spatial Model

Duncan Black and Anthony Downs, two pioneers in the study of social choice, introduced models with continuous sets of alternatives in social choice theory. If a committee has to decide how much money to spend on foreign aid, for example, the alternatives range from a low of zero to a high number equaling the whole budget. There are many modelers who think of the space of political alternatives as an ideological continuum from liberal to conservative (see Hinich and Munger, 1994). The options, whether they are the promises of political candidates or bills before a legislature, are rightly given geometrical structure and insight by the spatial model.

A **unidimensional spatial model** has a "policy space" or "space of alternatives" drawn from the real number line, $X \subseteq \Re$. The "real number line," the set of all real numbers between $-\infty$ and $+\infty$, is typically referred to by a symbol like $\Re$ or $\mathbb{R}$, depending what is convenient for the typist. Because the alternatives are real numbers, it is meaningful to consider, for example, whether policy x is more desirable than some combination of x and y, such as $\lambda x + (1 - \lambda)y$. The coefficient λ (the Greek lambda) varies between 0 and 1.

In the **multidimensional spatial model**, the space of alternatives is drawn from a multidimensional space, $X \subseteq \Re^m$. This means that each alternative has m coordinates. It is called an m-dimensional space. For example, if a committee is deciding on spending levels for foreign aid and food stamps, an alternative is a point in a two-dimensional space, $\Re^2$. To be thorough, note that $\Re^2 = \{(x_1, x_2) \mid x_1 \in \Re \text{ and } x_2 \in \Re\}$. This may be more familiar to readers as the Cartesian plane, or X-Y plane, that is treated in high school algebra.

The term $\mathfrak{R}^2$ is pronounced "R-two," not "R-squared," even though the latter might seem appropriate in light of the fact that $\mathfrak{R}^2 = \mathfrak{R} \times \mathfrak{R}$, the Cartesian product of $\mathfrak{R}$ with $\mathfrak{R}$. If there are nine spending programs, then the policy alternatives are coordinates in a nine-dimensional space. It is hard to image a graph of such a space, but it is easy enough to write $\mathfrak{R}^9$ to refer to the Cartesian product of nine real number lines, i.e.,

$$\mathfrak{R}^9 = \left\{ (x_1, x_2, x_3, x_4, x_5, x_6, x_7, x_8, x_9) \mid x_j \in \mathfrak{R} \text{ for } j = 1, \ldots, 9 \right\}$$

The policy space is a subset of this nine-dimensional space, so $X \subseteq \mathfrak{R}^9$. Each proposed alternative must specify a value for each of the nine dimensions. When a policy space is built by combining real number lines in this way, it is called a **Euclidean space**.

Utility Functions

In a spatial model, we are given not only a space of alternatives, but also the preferences of the voters. The basic specification is a binary preference relation, R_i, which has the same meaning as it did in the discrete case. However, in order to take advantage of the mathematical power inherent in the real numbers, it is usually necessary to represent a voter's preference relation, R_i, by an **ordinal utility function**, U_i. An ordinal utility function assigns a numerical value to each alternative, so that the alternative that is more appealing has a higher utility value.

The use of a utility function does not add any information above and beyond the weak preference relation. Rather, it is merely a new mathematical representation of the preferences that are given in R_i. The preference relation R_i can be represented by an **ordinal utility function** $U_i: X \to \mathfrak{R}$ if for any pair of alternatives, x and y,

$$x R_i y \quad \text{if and only if} \quad U_i(x) \geq U_i(y)$$

This is the *representability criterion*. If R_i is representable by a utility function, then for any alternative x, there is a real number $U_i(x)$ that is associated with it. Obviously, if $x I_i y$, then $U_i(x) = U_i(y)$, and if $x P_i y$, then $U_i(x) > U_i(y)$. Furthermore, since $U_i(x)$ and $U_i(y)$ are real numbers, then the relations R_i, I_i, and P_i defined on X are comparable to $\geq$, $=$, and $>$ on the real numbers. If we are given a weak preference relation, we know that there is a nonempty set of **maximal elements,**

$$\{x \in X \mid \forall y \in X, x R_i y\}$$

If there is only one maximal element, then it is the voter's **ideal point,** typically denoted x_i^*.

The term "ordinal" in "ordinal utility function" means that a utility function U_i is not a unique representation of R_i. Any "order-preserving transformation" of U_i is also a representation of the voter's preferences. If U_i represents a preference relation, so will $3 * U_i$, $\sqrt{U_i(x)}$, or $\log(U_i)$ because the ranking of the alternatives is not affected by these transformations. The absolute size of the utility numbers assigned is irrelevant to the representation. If, on one utility scale, the utilities of x and y are 3 and 10, then y is preferred to x. If the scale is multiplied by 1 million, then x will have a utility of 3 million and y will be worth 10 million. After the transformation, y is still preferred to x. No important results in the theory should depend on the specific numerical values of the utility function.

The advantage of the utility function approach is that we can use the tools of Cartesian geometry and calculus (or more advanced methods, such as topology or real analysis) to investigate voter behavior. A utility function for a unidimensional policy space is depicted in Figure 4.1. The dimension is called X. Specific alternatives in X are referred to as $x \in X$. The utility function is drawn as a

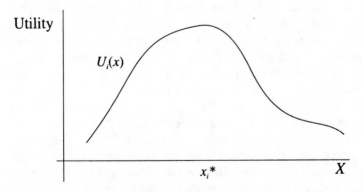

Figure 4.1. Single-Peaked Preferences in One Dimension

continuous, **single-peaked** function that attains its maximum when $x = x_i^*$. As policy moves away from x_i^*, the utility is reduced. Note, as illustrated, there is no assumption of symmetry in the utility function.

In Figure 4.2, the geometrical depiction for a two-dimensional policy space is introduced. In that figure, the two policy dimensions are called X_1 and X_2. In the top panel, the two-dimensional space of alternatives is shown and the utility function is drawn so that the more attractive policies have higher utility values. The voter's ideal point is $x_i^* = (x_{i1}^*, x_{i2}^*)$. (The first subscript refers to the voter; the second refers to the dimension.) Because it is difficult to draw in three dimensions, the representation in the bottom panel of Figure 4.2 is more frequently used. The figure also includes some indifference curves. An **indifference curve** is defined as a set of points that are equally desirable—the individual is indifferent among them. As policy proposals shift away from the ideal point, the voter is moved onto progressively "lower" (less attractive) indifference curves. The indifference curves are drawn as smooth ovals for illustrative purposes, but without more detailed assumptions about preferences (see below), there is no reason to expect that they could not be kinked or irregular in shape.

If we assume x_i^* exists in the interior of X, then the indifference curves of less desirable points encircle x_i^*. Readers who have studied microeconomics might be startled to see these preferences because microeconomic models are often constructed around the notion of nonsatiability (or monotonicity). Political preferences are usually assumed with interior ideal points. If the space is thought of as an ideological spectrum, it seems only natural that people can have ideal points in the interior of the space. (There are moderates, after all!) In some models of budgeting, the fact that there is a finite amount of money to spend causes an implicit tradeoff between policies, thus causing a voter to arrive at a most preferred spending combination (for more details, see Ordeshook, 1986).

In addition to the power of the geometrical illustration, we can use the tools of mathematics to investigate the behavior of a voter with a given utility function. Calculus can be used, for example, to find x_i^* by maximizing $U_i(x)$, possibly subject to constraints. The model can also be used to find the directions in which policy might move away from x that will increase the level of utility. In Figures 4.1 and 4.2, the utility function is drawn as a smooth, unbroken line or surface.

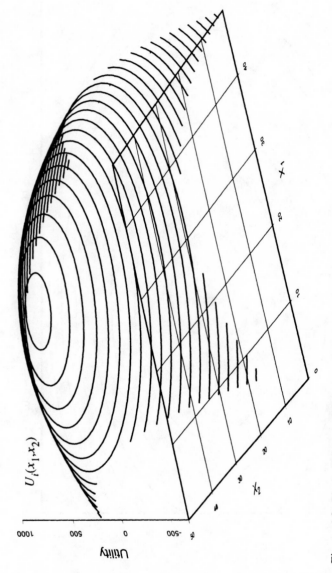

$U_i(x_1, x_2)$

Utility

Figure 4.2. Single-Peaked Preferences in Two Dimensions (continued)

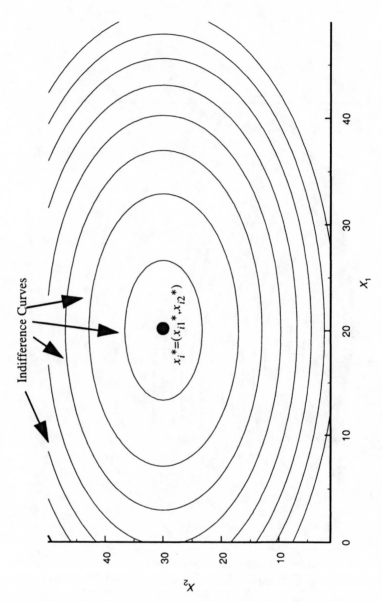

Figure 4.2. (continued)

When a function is continuous, as drawn, we can imagine a process of gradual "hill-climbing," gradual movement toward the ideal point. It is important to investigate the possibility that a voter might have preferences R_i that lead to a workable utility representation of that sort. The investigation of this problem takes us into a consideration of some ideas from a field of mathematics known as real analysis.

Continuity and Utility Representations on the Continuum

Not all preferences will lead to workable utility functions. There is no guarantee that a continuous utility representation of the voter's preferences will exist, even if preferences are transitive and complete. Additional assumptions about R_i are required before we can state with any confidence that a utility function is continuous or that indifference curves are smooth ovals.

One of the many contributions of Nobel Prize winning economist Gerard Debreu (1959) was a formalization of the idea of continuity for a preference relation and the proof that a continuous utility function does exist if the preference relation satisfies his requirement for continuity. To develop this idea, it is first necessary to define the concepts of open and closed sets. Readers are no doubt familiar with the closed interval [0, 1], which includes its endpoints, 0 and 1. If we lopped off the endpoints only, we would have the open interval (0, 1). The set (0, 1) includes numbers that get very close to 0 and 1, such as 0.0000001 and 0.99999999, but it does not include the 0 or 1. It might seem that removing the endpoints changes only trivially the mathematical properties of the set, but the effect is really quite large. For example, the question "what is the largest number in [0, 1]?" has an answer, but the same is not true of (0, 1).

For mathematical generality, it is not sufficient to define an open set as a closed set with the endpoints lopped off, but we would not be going too badly. The basic idea of an open set is that no point in the set lies on a boundary. There is a workable formalization that does not take too much effort. Consider a set of points X drawn from $\mathfrak{R}^m$. Openness means that no matter how close you pick a point x to the boundary of the set, one can draw a ball around x and the entirety of the ball fits within the set. More formally, let's use the expression $d(x, y)$ as a measure of distance between two points.

Define the ε-ball (pronounced epsilon ball) B_ε around a point x as the set of all points y within distance ε from x, or $d(x, y) < \varepsilon$. Formally, the ε-ball is

$$B_\varepsilon(x) = \{y \in X \mid d(x, y) < \varepsilon\}$$

A set X is **open** if for each $x \in X$, no matter how close to the "edge," there is a number ε small enough so that the epsilon-ball $B_\varepsilon(x)$ is contained entirely within X. This general definition of openness obviously works with open intervals such as $(0, 1)$, but its advantage is that it works in higher dimensions as well.

The concept of a closed set is defined in terms of the open set. Consider $B \subseteq X$. The complement of B, written $X - B$ or B^c, is the set of all points in X that are not in B. B is **closed** if the complement of B is open.

If you don't like that definition of a closed set, consider this one. A **closed set** is one that contains all of its limit points. This definition is more complicated, but in introducing it we can touch on the ideas of sequences and limits. A **sequence** in $X \subseteq \mathfrak{R}^m$ is an infinite set of points, $\{x^1, x^2, \ldots\}$, that can be put in one-to-one correspondence with the natural numbers (those are the counting numbers, 1, 2, 3, $\ldots$, ∞). A sequence $\{x^1, x^2, x^3, \ldots\}$ might be referred to as $\{x^j\}$ for short, and an arbitrary element in the sequence is referred to as x^j. The sequence can wander through X in any way you choose. However, if you choose the sequence so its successive points get closer and closer to a point x, then the sequence **converges** to x. Mathematically $\{x^j\}$ converges to x if, for any $\varepsilon > 0$, there is an integer q such that $\forall j > q$, $x^j \in B_\varepsilon(x)$. Verbally, for any ε you pick, there is some point in the sequence, say x^q, after which all points in the sequence are no further than ε from x. For example, the sequence $\{1/i\} = \{1, 1/2, 1/3, 1/4, \ldots\}$ converges to 0. The point to which a sequence converges is called a **limit** or a "limit point," which is written as $x^j \to x$. A closed set is one that includes all limit points, meaning that any point to which a sequence in X converges is also in X. This is illustrated in Figure 4.3.

Debreu used the notion of a closed set to describe his idea of continuity to a preference relation. For any $x \in X$, the set of points that is as desirable as x is

$$R_i(x) = \{y \in X \mid y R_i x\}$$

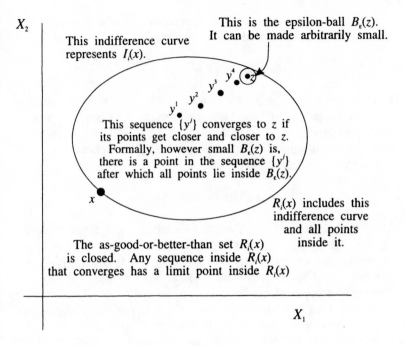

Figure 4.3. Continuous Preference Relations

This set $R_i(x)$ might be called the **as-good-or-better-than set**. Similarly, Debreu defined the as-bad-or-worse-than set, $R_i^{-1}(x)$:

$$R_i^{-1}(x) = \{ y \in X \mid x R_i y \}$$

Debreu defined a **continuous preference relation** as one in which both $R_i(x)$ and $R_i^{-1}(x)$ are closed sets.

Debreu's idea of a continuous preference relation aims to capture the intuition that preferences do not change abruptly in response to minor changes in policies being considered. If we pick points that wander around in the as-good-or-better-than set of a point x, then any point that we can get close to ought to be as-good-or-better-than x. More formally, if we are given a sequence $\{x^j\}$ in $R_i(x)$ that converges to a point z (i.e., $x^j \to z$), then it must be that $z R_i x$.

Note, it would be mathematically equivalent to define continuity in terms of an open **preferred-to set**,

$$P_i(x) = \{y \in X \mid y P_i x\}$$

$P_i(x)$ is the complement of a closed set $R_i^{-1}(x)$, so $P_i(x)$ must be open—by definition! If $P_i(x)$ is open, it means that one can pick any point preferred to x, such as z, and there are points "all around z" that are also preferred to x. While we are on the subject, we should define the indifferent-to set of x,

$$I_i(x) = \{y \in X \mid x I_i y\}$$

The set I_i is more commonly called an indifference curve. Note that the set $R_i(x) = I_i(x) \cup P_i(x)$. The indifferent-to set is the boundary of the as-good-or-better-than set in most cases (such as Figure 4.3).

After one final mathematical detail, we will be ready to state Debreu's theorem. A set X is said to be **connected** if it cannot be represented as the union of two disjoint, nonempty, open sets. There's no way to "cut apart" a connected set without separating points that are "touching," in the sense that, at the point of the cut, the smallest possible ε-ball includes points in both of the sets. The interval [0, 1] is a connected set, for example.

Theorem (Debreu, 1959, p. 56). Let $X \subseteq R^n$ be connected and R_i be a complete and transitive weak preference ordering on X. If R_i is continuous, then there exists a continuous function $U_i\colon X \to \Re$ that represents R_i.

This is an important theorem because it justifies our models, which depict choice as if it were the maximization of a utility function. We can call on results from calculus to assert that a maximum value of utility can be found for a continuous utility function defined on a closed interval (Weierstrass's theorem).

Is the assumption that preferences are continuous a strong, unrealistic one? Most social choice modelers don't think so, but there is always room for disagreement. Before the assumption is rejected because it is too unrealistic, one should consider the results to which the theory leads. If continuity is the linchpin in the derivation of a result that seems unbelievable, then the next step ought to be a weakening of the assumption. By testing the "sensitivity" of the results, one obtains a better idea of the role of the assumption.

Convexity and Single-Peakedness

We have found conditions under which a functional representation of utility exists, but what would it look like? Is it a workable mathematical model? Does the utility function have a maximum? Is the ideal point unique? Are the indifference curves smooth? Consideration of these questions takes us to a discussion of the critical terms "convexity" and "quasi-concavity."

Everything is simpler in a unidimensional model. We can discuss points, such as x, y, and z, and also work with them as real numbers. In that vein, preferences are said to be single-peaked if, whenever $y, z < x_i^*$ or $y, z > x_i^*$, $|y - x_i^*| < |z - x_i^*|$ implies $y P_i x$. (Verbalize this term by term: whenever y and z are on the same side of x_i^*, if y is closer than z to x_i^*, then y is preferred z.) Single-peakedness requires that a voter has a favorite, and that voter would rather have policy move toward the favorite than away from it. This is easily translated into a utility function, $U_i(x)$, the value of which declines as policy moves away from the ideal point. This definition excludes the possibility of indifference between two adjacent points.

When we turn to the multidimensional spatial model, it is not so simple to capture the idea of single-peakedness in a workable mathematical model. A first guess is to assume that the utility function is concave, meaning "cupped downward." That guess turns out to be wrong, however. Instead, a utility function that is single-peaked is strictly quasi-concave, which in turn implies that the preferred-to set, $P_i(x)$, is a convex set.

It is necessary to begin with the fundamental terms "convex combination" and "convex set." A **convex combination** of two points x and y is a weighted average $\lambda x + (1 - \lambda)y$. The weighting parameter λ can vary from 0 to 1 (write $\lambda \in [0, 1]$). When $\lambda = 0$, the convex combination is equal to y. When $\lambda = 1$, the convex combination reduces to x. As λ is increased from 0 and 1, as illustrated in Figure 4.4, the convex combination travels along a line from y to x. The idea of a convex combination arises in many mathematical models, so it is worth taking a minute to examine the figure.

42

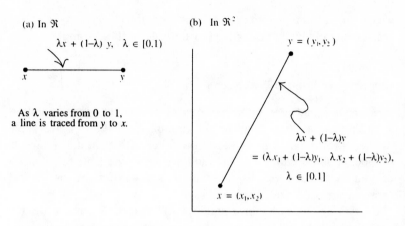

(a) In $\Re$

$$\lambda x + (1-\lambda) \, y, \quad \lambda \in [0,1)$$

$x \qquad\qquad y$

As λ varies from 0 to 1,
a line is traced from y to x.

(b) In $\Re^2$

$y = (y_1, y_2)$

$$\lambda x + (1-\lambda)y$$
$$= (\lambda x_1 + (1-\lambda)y_1, \; \lambda x_2 + (1-\lambda)y_2),$$
$$\lambda \in [0,1]$$

$x = (x_1, x_2)$

(c) A convex set

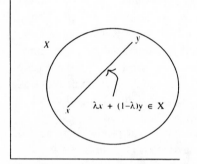

X

y

$\lambda x + (1-\lambda)y \in X$

A set that is not convex

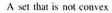
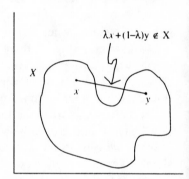

$\lambda x + (1-\lambda)y \notin X$

X

$x \qquad\qquad y$

Figure 4.4. Convex Combinations

Given a working knowledge of convex combinations, the notion of
a convex set should be easy to understand. Informally, a convex set is
one such that a straight line connecting any two points in the set is
also in the set. Technically, convexity requires $\forall x, \; y \in X, \; \{(\lambda x + (1 - \lambda)y) \mid \lambda \in [0, 1]\} \subset X$. This definition applies to any Euclidean
space. Since the idea of convexity is extremely important at several
future points in the analysis, do not gloss over it at this stage!

Debreu applied the idea of convex sets and convex combinations to
develop a categorization of workable preference relations. In his

43

approach (Debreu, 1959, pp. 59–61), preferences might be weakly convex, convex, or strictly convex. Each category is illustrated in Figure 4.5.

Preferences are **weakly convex** if $x R_i y$ then $\lambda x + (1 - \lambda)y R_i y$, $\forall \lambda \in [0, 1]$. If x is as good as y, any convex combination of x and y

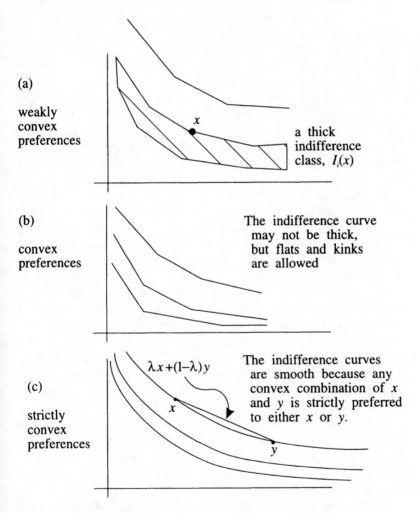

Figure 4.5. Debreu's Typology of Convex Preference Relations

is as good as y. This definition allows the possibility that $I_i(x)$ is a "thick" indifference class. Even this weak convexity is strong enough to assure that the preferred-to set of x, $P_i(x)$, is a convex set.

Preferences are **convex** if $xP_i y$ then $\lambda x + (1 - \lambda)y \ P_i \ y$, $\forall \lambda \in (0, 1]$. In other words, if voter i likes one thing more than another, that voter will accept a weighted average of the two in place of the less desirable offering. This definition guarantees us that the indifference class $I_i(x)$ is a curve, rather than a "thick" region. This assures us that x is on the boundary of $P_i(x)$, so that even the smallest movement away from x (in the right direction, of course) will be preferred. However, it does not rule out the possibility of "flat" segments in the indifference curves.

Preferences are **strictly convex** if $xI_i y$ then $\lambda x + (1 - \lambda)y \ P_i \ x$, $\forall \lambda \in (0, 1)$. Any point along a line between x and y is more appealing than either x or y. Strict convexity assures us that $R_i(x)$ has no "sharp edges" or "kinks." This kind of convexity is necessary to assure us that the indifference curves have their smooth, oval appearance.

To make sure the definitions are clear, the reader should study them until the following claim is believable. Convexity and strict convexity assure that if a maximal element exists, it is unique, so there is an ideal point. Furthermore, if a given preference relation R_i is strictly convex, it is also convex, and one that is convex is also weakly convex.

If a preference relation is convex, then it has the property of single-peakedness that we are seeking to represent. Intuitively, when indifference curves are thin and the preferred-to set is convex, that means we can pick a point x, and then improve on it by moving to a point y, in the direction of the ideal point. This is illustrated in Figure 4.6. Then we can move again into the preferred-to set of y, and so forth, until we reach the ideal point. Because the preference relation is convex, the preferred-to sets are nested within each other.

If we want to describe a utility function that represents convex preferences, how do we go about it? The first guess that one might have is that $U_i(x)$ is concave, but after some analysis, we find instead that $U_i(x)$ must satisfy a slightly more complicated requirement known as strict quasi-concavity.

The starting place for a derivation of this result is a review of the idea of a concave function. As the reader may recall, a function is

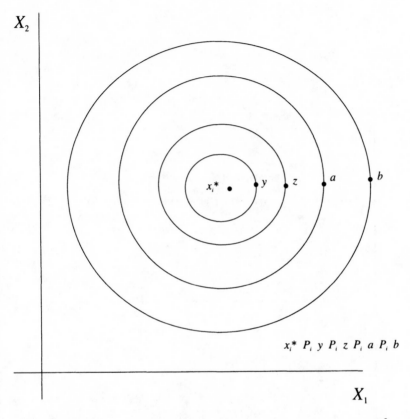

$x_i^* P_i y P_i z P_i a P_i b$

Figure 4.6. Strictly Convex Preferences with x_i^* in the Interior of $x \subseteq \Re^2$

said to be concave if it is "cupped downward." Technically, this can be expressed in the language of convex combinations:

$f: X \rightarrow R$ is **strictly concave** if $\forall x_1, x_2 \in X$ and $\lambda \in (0, 1)$,

$$f(\lambda x_1 + (1 - \lambda)x_2) > \lambda f(x_1) + (1 - \lambda)f(x_2)$$

(Repeat this to yourself three times: The function of the convex combination is greater than the convex combination of values of the function.) A concave function is drawn in Figure 4.7a.

(a)

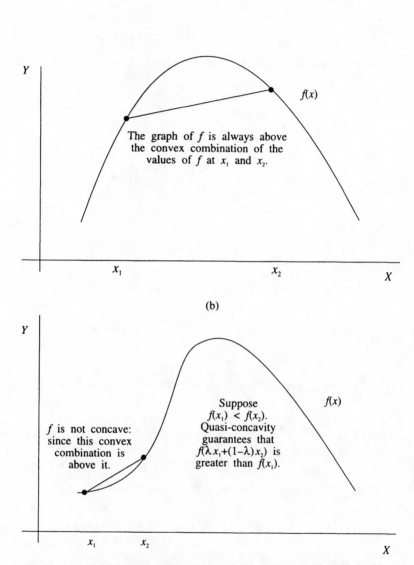

The graph of f is always above the convex combination of the values of f at x_1 and x_2.

(b)

Suppose $f(x_1) < f(x_2)$. Quasi-concavity guarantees that $f(\lambda x_1 + (1-\lambda) x_2)$ is greater than $f(x_1)$.

f is not concave: since this convex combination is above it.

Figure 4.7. Concavity and Strict Quasi-Concavity (a) A Strictly Concave Function (b) A Quasi-Concave Function

The ordinal utility theory does not, unfortunately, assure us that utility functions will be concave. The reason for this is that the utility function may be subjected to any order-preserving transformation, even transformations that change the concavity of the function. The best we can expect is for the utility function to be "quasi-concave." Quasi-concavity is preserved by order-preserving transformations. A quasi-concave function is illustrated in Figure 4.7b. Quasi-concavity can be defined in either of two ways. The first, and undoubtedly the simplest definition, is

$U_i: X \to \Re$ is **quasi-concave** if for all $a \in \Re$, the set
$\{x \in X: U_i(x) \geq a\}$ is convex. This means that the
as-good-or-better-than set $R_i(x)$ is convex, since U_i
represents R_i

The second, and equivalent definition of quasi-concavity, is more comparable to the definition of concavity above:

$U_i: X \to \Re$ is **quasi-concave** if $\forall x_1, x_2 \in X$ and $\lambda \in (0,1)$,

$$U_i(\lambda x_1 + (1 - \lambda)x_2) \geq \min\{U_i(x_1), U_i(x_2)\}$$

(Repeat to yourself: The utility of a convex combination of two points is greater than the utility of the least desirable point.) A function is said to be **strictly quasi-concave** if the $\geq$ sign is replaced by $>$ in this definition.

This analysis establishes the following claims:

1. If a preference relation is weakly convex, then the utility function representing it is quasi-concave.
2. If a preference relation is convex, then the utility function representing it is strictly quasi-concave.

In a research article, one will typically find preferences defined either as a binary relation or as a utility function, not both. The choice is made for technical and presentational reasons, not because one method of describing preferences is superior to the other. The two models are describing the same thing in different terminology. If a mathematical result is obtained more easily by representing preferences as a binary relation (along with the attendant preferred-to sets), then that route should be followed. If, on the other hand, some mathematical methods that can be applied to utility functions make a result easier to derive, then research should proceed along that route. A researcher is not making a stronger assumption by stating a model in terms of a utility function than by stating it in terms of a convex preference relation. Mathematical convenience is the only real reason to pursue one method of analysis or another.

5. THE UNIDIMENSIONAL SPATIAL MODEL

The spatial model of voting addresses, among other things, the conditions under which the majority rule voting cycles are limited to a top-cycle set or eliminated altogether. We consider (for the most part) **binary agendas**: voting procedures that compare two alternatives at a time. The unidimensional model with single-peaked preferences leads to the most encouraging results in the spatial theory of majority.

The Importance of Single-Peaked Preferences

In Downs' (1957) classic book, *An Economic Theory of Democracy*, the space of alternatives is thought of as an ideological spectrum in which political candidates (representing parties) take positions. Downs (1957, p. 116) argued, "If we assume that the left end of the scale represents full government control [of the economy], and the right end means a completely free market, we can rank parties by their views on this issue in a way that might be nearly universally recognized as accurate." While he admitted that the political space is in fact more complicated, Downs argued that the analytical benefits far outweighed the inaccuracy of the model. Similarly, Black's (1958) seminal research on committee decision-making also explored the importance of single-peaked preferences. To these authors and many others who have followed in their footsteps, a reasonable person is someone who has a favorite and becomes progressively more disappointed as the social choice moves away from that favorite policy. The assumption of single-peakedness is typically invoked, not by an appeal to transitivity or pure rationality, but rather by an appeal to taste or empirical verisimilitude. As such, single-peakedness is a modeling assumption, not a derivation or intrinsic result from rationality. Single-peakedness is both mathematically workable and, at least in the eyes of social choice theorists, a reasonable description of how people are (or ought to be).

Recall that a voter is assumed to have **ideal point**, or most-preferred point, x_i^*. The ideal point, if it exists, is a member of this set:

$$\{x \in X \mid x R_i y \; \forall y \in X\}$$

Single-peakedness means that the desirability of a proposal declines as it moves away from x_i^* in either direction.

The reader should recall that single-peakedness does not imply symmetry. Symmetry would imply that a person prefers y to z if y is closer to the point. Single-peaked preferences can be skewed, so that points further away from x_i^* on one side may be preferred to points that are closer to x_i^* on the other side.

The Median Voter Theorem

This theorem is one of the most important results in social choice theory. The median voter theorem states conditions under which majority rule leads to a transitive social preference ordering. It is usually attributed to Black (1958).

Median Voter Theorem. If N is odd and preferences are single-peaked in one dimension, then (1) the median of the voters' ideal points is a Condorcet winner and (2) majority rule leads to a transitive social preference ordering.

Proof. As many have noted (Ordeshook, 1986, p. 162; Enelow and Hinich, 1984a), the proof of part 1 is quite simple. Suppose the voters are numbered in order, so that the voter with the lowest ideal point is voter number 1, the next highest ideal point belongs to voter number 2, etc. The median ideal point belongs to the voter numbered $M = (n + 1)/2$. (With three voters, the median is 2; with seven voters it is 4, etc.) Given the median point, x_M^*, consider a proposal $x > x_M^*$ which is to the right of x_M^*. Obviously, the median voter M will oppose the move away from x_M^*. Because preferences are single-peaked, the voters whose ideal points are to the left of x_M^* will also oppose the move to the right. Hence, by a majority vote, x_M^* will defeat movements in any direction.

The proof of part 2, transitivity, requires just a bit of finesse. It is necessary to show that xPy and yPz imply xPz. This is easy if x, y, and z all lie on the same side of x_M^*. If so, x is closer to x_M^* than z. If x and y are on one side and z is on the other, the reader has to have a little imagination. Obviously, since xPy, x is closer to the median than y. If under majority rule yPz, then any point in the interval (x_M^*, y) will be preferred to z. The point x is closer to x_M^* than y, so x must be preferred to z. QED

To illustrate importance of single-peakedness, consider the three voter–three alternative example that was discussed previously and illustrated in Figure 3.2. It was observed that the majority cycle arose in 2 of 36 cases—preference profiles 23 and 28. In Figure 5.1b, the utility functions that represent profile 23 are drawn. Note that voter 3's preferences are not single-peaked. The reader can verify that no matter how one might arrange x, y, and z along the horizontal axis, there is no way to make all three of the utility functions single-peaked. On the other hand, preferences are single-peaked in Figure 5.1a, which represents profile 34. It is easy to verify that the median of the

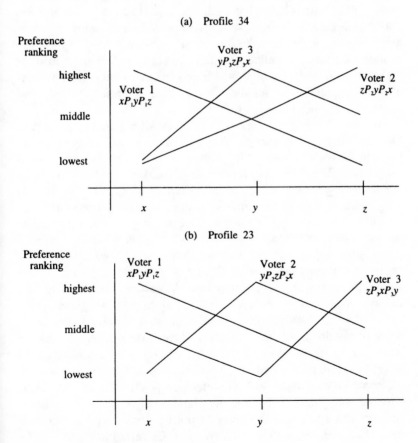

Figure 5.1. Utility Representations

ideal points in Figure 5.1a is indeed a Condorcet winner and that majority rule generates a transitive ordering of x, y, and z.

Single-peakedness is a sufficient condition for a Condorcet winner to exist, but it is not a necessary condition. This fact is often overlooked. If one added 1000 voters with non-single-peaked preferences like those of voter 3 to Figure 5.1b, then z would be a Condorcet winner. Single-peakedness guarantees a stable outcome in the center of the electorate, but it is not required.

The median voter theorem is used in many contexts. The critical question is the believability of the single-peakedness assumption. If X represents the amount of money to be spent on a program, then it is not difficult to believe that each voter would have an ideal point and that deviations from it would reduce the voter's utility. Presumably, spending more than the ideal would imply disutility in the form of increased taxes or deficit spending. Sometimes X is thought of as an ideological spectrum upon which people have ideal points. Moderates are happiest with middle policies, liberals prefer the left, and conservatives prefer the right.

Probably the most famous use of the one-dimensional model is in Downs' (1957) *An Economic Theory of Democracy*. Downs describes two candidates choosing policy platforms (Downs called them political parties). Voter preferences are single-peaked and the candidates are solely motivated by the desire to obtain office. The voters may not abstain. Under these conditions, the policy platforms of the two candidates will converge to the median of the voter ideal points. As soon as one candidate adopts the median voter's ideal point as a policy proposal, the other has no choice but to go for a tie by choosing the same position, or else be sure to lose the election. The competitive pressure of majority rule draws the candidates toward identical positions in the center of the electorate, a tendency that Downs thought was surprising (and somewhat perverse). The same sorts of results have been found in economic studies of location decisions by firms (Hotelling, 1929; Smithies, 1941). Many studies have followed in Downs' tradition, hoping to find the conditions under which candidates will separate their positions. Factors such as variable voter turnout, uncertainty about voter preferences, political primary processes, and the entry of third parties have been considered (Ledyard, 1981, 1984; Palfrey, 1984; Calvert, 1985; Cox, 1987a; Shepsle, 1991).

The median voter theorem has also been very influential in studies of decision-making in committees and legislatures. When preferences are single-peaked and the voters are allowed to propose alternatives freely, then the median of the ideal points should be the winning proposal. Once the median ideal point is proposed, it cannot be defeated, at least if everyone votes and everyone votes sincerely. Since the median is such a dominant position, some researchers will simply assume that the group choice is the median. This may be a dangerous practice if the methods of decision-making do not match the assumptions behind the theorem, as is illustrated in the next section.

Reversion Points and Take-It-or-Leave-It Offers

When preferences are single-peaked, particularly interesting models to describe constrained choices can be constructed. Begin by supposing that there is an agenda-setter who can ask the voters for approval to implement a proposal y. If no majority grants permission, then policy reverts to a predesignated setting, r. This predesignated policy, known as a **reversion point**, can have a great deal of impact on the behavior of the voters. Basically, the results indicate that if the reversion point is undesirable to the voters, then the agenda-setter can use the threat of the reversion point to force voters to accept policies that would not otherwise be acceptable. In particular, the agenda-setter can force the majority to accept policy that is far from the median.

Figure 5.2 illustrates one single-peaked preference curve for a voter i. The most desirable policy would be x_i^*, of course, and i would vote for that if it were offered. Suppose, however, that the agenda-setter offered policy y^1. (The superscripts are used to distinguish different policy proposals.) Would i vote in favor of y^1? It all depends on what will happen if y^1 is rejected. The figure is drawn with three possible reversion points, which are labeled r^0, r^1, and r^2. If the reversion point is r^0, voter i is worse off with y^1 and so i will vote no. If the reversion point is r^1, then i will see that y^1 is more attractive than r^1 and i will vote yes. That's the perverse logic of politics with reversion points. If the reversion point is made less desirable, moved from r^0 to r^1, for example, then a voter who would not have supported y^1 is forced to do so. The reversion point r^2 is

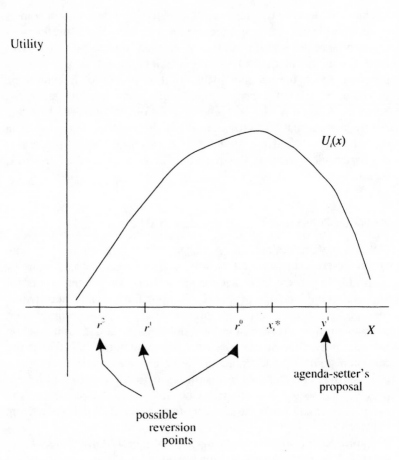

Figure 5.2. A Take-It-or-Leave-It Offer

less desirable still. If r^2 is the reversion point, then i will vote yes on a policy that is even further from the ideal point than y^1.

Suppose the dimension X being discussed represents funding for a program, such as education. If the agenda-setter prefers to raise the program's budget, the impact of the reversion point is obvious. The agenda-setter can get i to support a budget higher than x_i^* because the reversion point is undesirable. By adding more single-peaked voters to a model of this type, the reader can easily verify what will happen in a majority rule setting. If the agenda-setter wants to increase a program above the median, it can be done if the reversion point is to the left of the median of the ideal points. On the other hand, if the reversion point is above the median, the agenda-setter will not be able to obtain majority approval for higher spending than the reversion point. For a review of the model and a discussion of its extensions, the reader should consult an excellent essay by Rosenthal (1990).

Reversion point politics arise in any situation in which one person or group, known as the agenda-setter, can make a take-it-or-leave-it proposal. If the reversion point is quite undesirable, then the agenda-setter can force a community of voters to accept policies that are far from their ideal points. A classic article by Romer and Rosenthal (1978) first presented this model and worked out many of its details. Their subsequent empicial research explored a law in Oregon which gave the local school board the power to propose school funding bills. If the bill was rejected, school funding reverted to the 1916 funding level. Districts formed since 1916 thus reverted to 0 when the school bill was rejected. One would expect, and the data show, that the agenda-setters are more successful in raising budgets above the median in the newer districts where the 0 reversion level applies (see Rosenthal, 1990, and studies cited therein). The same logic is applicable in many circumstances. The common element is that if an agenda-setter's proposal is rejected, a reversion policy takes effect. In models of presidential vetoes, for example, the president can reject a law proposed by Congress and policy reverts to the status quo. Congress can exploit the undesirability of the status quo to force the president to accept a policy that is far from the presidential ideal point (see Kiewiet and McCubbins, 1988; Ingberman and Yao, 1991).

Unraveling in Democratically Governed Groups

In the reversion point model, it is supposed that some policy can be imposed on all voters if the agenda-setter's proposal is rejected. Suppose, on the other hand, we are considering a voluntary organization, one from which voters can withdraw when the group choice displeases them. Obviously, nothing can be imposed on these voters that is worse than exit from the group. As it turns out, each voter's exit utility level acts to define a personal reversion point.

Suppose, at least at the outset, that there is no agenda-setter and that group policies are determined by majority rule. This "exit model" of decision-making in voluntary organizations is discussed in Johnson (1990, 1996). Figure 5.3 illustrates voter i's utility function $U_i(x)$ and the exit utility k_i. The level k_i is the happiness of i after withdrawing from the organization or group. The dimension X might be any group policy or its dues level. Below the utility function, there is a "tolerable interval," T_i, to represent the set of all group policies that are tolerable to voter i. Note also that voter i's ideal point is represented by a tick on the tolerable interval. Considering a policy

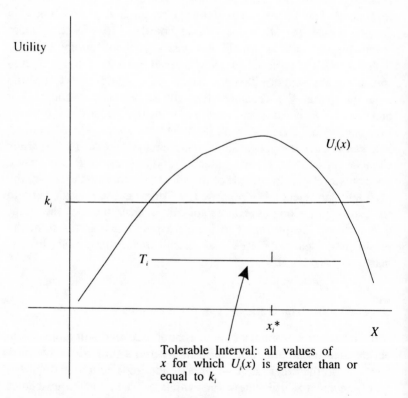

Figure 5.3. Exit Utility and Group Membership

y^1, if $U_i(y^1) \geq k_i$, which implies $y^1 \in T_i$, voter i will remain in the group.

The membership of a group is stable if the group's policy $y^1 \in T_i \ \forall i \in N$. This is a somewhat demanding criterion. Either voters must be similar in their tastes or they must be tolerant of group policies that differ from their ideal points. Preferences for five voters are drawn in Figure 5.4a. The utility functions in Figure 5.4a are ordinal preferences, so they can be scaled up and down as long as the ordering is preserved. These utility functions have been scaled so that all participants have the same level of exit utility, k (that is, $k = k_1 = k_2 = k_3 = k_4 = k_5$). After this rescaling, a horizontal line through the voter preferences can be drawn, and the tolerable intervals in Figure 5.4b "fall out" as a result. The median of the ideal points is x_3^*. The reader will note, however, that this point is not tolerable to voter 1. If the group settles on the median policy by a majority vote, say, voter 1 will quit the group. This tendency of the median to be unacceptable to some members is called the unraveling problem. The way in which voluntary organizations deal with it has significant implications. For example, some groups will adopt rules that require unanimous consent to prevent the accidental expulsion of unhappy members. Others will allow leaders to set the agenda of the meeting, hoping to confine policies to those that are tolerable to all. If some of the members realize that voter 1 might quit, perhaps they will vote with care and assure that the outcome is tolerable to voter 1. Each of these situations can be modeled mathematically.

As a mathematical modeling exercise, it is interesting to study the difference between this model and the reversion point model. In the reversion point model, there is a "support interval," denoted by S_i. S_i includes the set of points x such that $U_i(x) \geq U_i(r^1)$. Using the preferences in Figure 5.5a (which duplicates Figure 5.4a) and the reversion point r^1 in that figure, we can calculate the support intervals of the five voters, as seen in Figure 5.5b. Notice that since the support interval necessarily includes the voter's ideal point, we can represent the ideal point by a tick mark on the support interval. The endpoints of the support intervals differ due to diversity of tastes among the voters. To raise spending above the median ideal point x_3^* as far as possible, the agenda-setter simply needs to propose the point y^1, which is the median of the right endpoints of the support intervals. Quite simply, the agenda-setter will choose the highest point that a majority prefers to the reversion point. Note that this

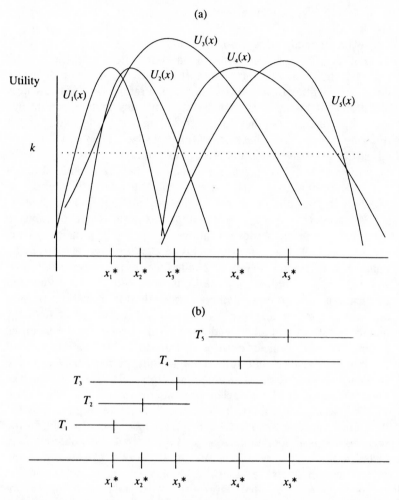

Figure 5.4. Preferences and Tolerable Intervals for Five Voters (a) Unraveling with Five Voters (b) Tolerable Intervals Derived from (a)

"median right endpoint" is not necessarily the highest support point of the median voter, although that is the case in Figure 5.5b.

As modeling enterprises, the reversion point model and the exit model are quite similar. In the exit model, the tolerable intervals are determined by passing a horizontal line through the utility functions.

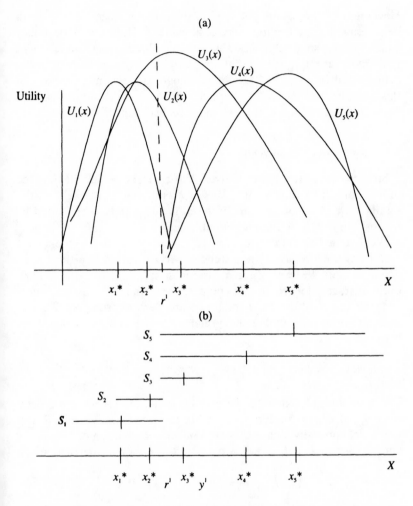

Figure 5.5. Reversion Point Politics (a) Preferences and Support Intervals for Five Voters (b) Support Intervals Derived from (a)

In the reversion point model, the support intervals are determined by drawing a vertical line above the reversion point through the utility functions. In the exit model, the voters' tolerable intervals need not overlap or have common endpoints. The reversion point model assures, at least, that one endpoint of the tolerable intervals is the same for all voters.

6. THE MULTIDIMENSIONAL SPATIAL MODEL

How many of the results obtained in the one-dimensional model can be extended to a multidimensional world? The model of policy conflict over a single dimension is certainly illuminating, but critics of the model are quick to point out that real life politics is more complicated (Stokes, 1963). Political debates involve many issues. In this section, we present the model that can be used to explore democratic government in these more realistic settings.

The Importance of Convexity

Suppose the space of alternatives X is a subset of Euclidean space of two or more dimensions. We are assuming that each of the significant aspects of a policy proposal is adequately represented by its position in the multidimensional space.

We assume there are voters $i = 1, \ldots, n$ and that these voters have "relatively well-behaved" preferences. At a most general and intuitively acceptable level, we can assume simply that there is a weak preference relation R_i that is complete and transitive. Strict preference P_i and indifference I_i relations are derived from R_i. We can take any point and define the **preferred-to set** and the **as-good-or-better-than set**:

$$P_i(x) = \{y \in X \mid y P_i x\} \qquad R_i(x) = \{y \in X \mid y R_i x\}$$

The most insight follows if we assume that preferences are strictly convex, but convex preferences lead to the same conclusions. Recall that strict convexity means that any convex combination of two points among which i is indifferent is preferred to either of the two points:

$$\text{If } x I_i y, \text{ then } \lambda x + (1 - \lambda) y P_i x$$

This assures us that the set $R_i(x)$ will have no flat portions or kinks in its outer boundary, a property which allows some mathematical insight below (see the discussion of utility gradients). Many of the central results of the multidimensional model can be obtained with less restrictive assumptions (see McKelvey, 1990).

In Figure 6.1, one voter's preferences are illustrated. The preference relation illustrated in the figure is assumed to be continuous [i.e., $P_i(x)$ is an open set]. The indifference curve including x, $I_i(x)$, is the boundary of the preferred-to set, and because of strict convexity it has the appearance of a smooth curve with no flat segments.

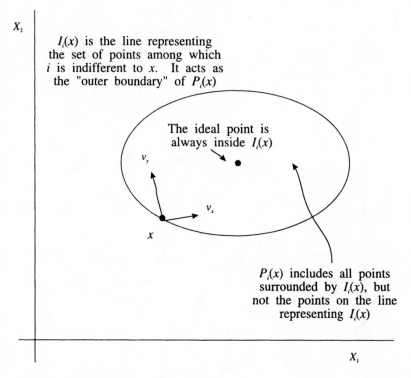

Figure 6.1. Strictly Convex Preferences

Examining the figure, we note that the voter will favor changes in the direction of any of the arrows that point away from x into the preferred-to set. (These arrows, labeled v_y, v_z, etc, represent vectors and we will discuss their importance below.) This is the most fundamental observation in the preliminary analysis of the multidimensional model, so don't pass over it lightly. Unless x happens to be the voter's ideal point, the preferred-to set of x contains many points (and perhaps more importantly, many directions away from x that would gain i's support).

Next consider two voters with strictly convex preferences in Figure 6.2. Considering again a point x, we see that the preferred-to sets of the two voters overlap. Both would favor a move from x to a point into the interior of the lens formed by the intersection of the

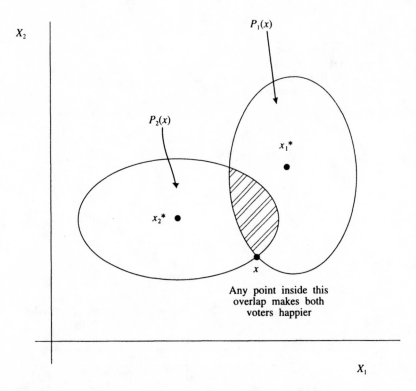

X_2

$P_1(x)$

$P_2(x)$

x_1^*

x_2^*

x

Any point inside this
overlap makes both
voters happier

X_1

Figure 6.2. Overlapping Preferred-to Sets of Voters 1 and 2

preferred-to sets. Almost all points in the two-dimensional model
have a nonempty intersection of this sort—two voters can find points
they would rather have. The exceptions—the ones from which the
two voters cannot agree to move—have a special property. These
points are in the **contract curve** between the two voters. A contact
curve is illustrated in Figure 6.3. Formally, the contract curve between two voters i and j is defined as

$$C_{ij} = \{ y \in X \mid \text{there does not exist } z \in X \text{ such that } z P_i y \text{ and } z P_j y \}$$

If the two voters were given the power to write a contract and choose
a policy that is jointly satisfactory, we would never expect them to
pick a point such as x. Instead, if they did reach an agreement, we

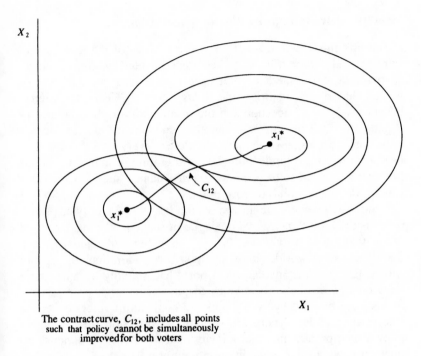

The contract curve, C_{12}, includes all points
such that policy cannot be simultaneously
improved for both voters

Figure 6.3. A Contract Curve for Voters 1 and 2

would expect it to be a point in the contract curve, such as z, a point
for which the intersection of the two preferred-to sets is empty.
(Readers with training in microeconomics will notice that the contract curve consists of points at which the indifference curves are
tangent to one another. That kind of detail need not bother other
readers.) The contract curve connects the ideal points of the two
voters.

The **Pareto set** (named in honor of the Italian welfare economist
Wilfredo Pareto) is analogous to the contract curve. A point is in the
Pareto set if there is no point that all voters prefer to it:

$$PAR = \{ y \in X \mid \text{there does not exist } z \in X \text{ such that } z P_i y \ \forall i \in N \}$$

For the same reason it seems logical to expect that two decision-
makers would choose a point in the contract curve, it is logical to
expect a group to choose a point in the Pareto set.

Stability Analysis: Majority Rule in Several Dimensions

The first fundamental question in the analysis of the multidimensional model is this: will one policy be undefeated? Is there a point, comparable to the median voter's ideal point in a one-dimensional model, that draws majority rule in its direction? This has been a heavily investigated question and the results indicate that the answer is generally no. I use the term **equilibrium point** to refer to such an unbeatable proposal—one that can defeat every other point in a head-on majority rule election. In the literature, equilibrium points have been referred to by a variety of other names, such as Condorcet winner, dominant point, or core point.

Intuitively, it seems the answer should be yes. Convexity of preferences is the multidimensional analogue of single-peakedness, and we found that single-peakedness brings a great deal of regularity in a one-dimensional world. However, upon reconsideration, the reader will realize that the median ideal point had stability because there were only two directions in which to go—left or right—and movements were blocked by evenly opposed numbers of voters on either side of the median. There are many more directions of movement away from a point x in a multidimensional world. In two dimensions, one can move away from x in an infinity of ways.

Let's consider the five voter example in Figure 6.4. Voter ideal points are labeled $x_1^*, x_2^*, x_3^*, x_4^*, x_5^*$. Pick a point x that is the ideal point of voter 1. Would a majority—three out of five voters—prefer to move policy away from x? We have to find out if there are points that are in the intersection of three voters' preferred-to sets. In this example, the cross-hatched region represents the points that are in the preferred-to sets of three or more voters. Obviously, there are points that a majority will choose over x.

How could x be an equilibrium, or unbeatable point? Excellent early papers by Plott (1967) and Davis, Degroot, and Hinich (1972) found conditions for the existence of an equilibrium point. The conditions offer some very deep insights in the (in)stability of multidimensional majority rule. More recent treatments have used different mathematical techniques to reach conclusions that support these findings, but also offer new results and insights. There are three predominant approaches to consider. The first characterization emphasizes the contract curves of the voters. The second explores a special case of voters with circular preferences. The third approach

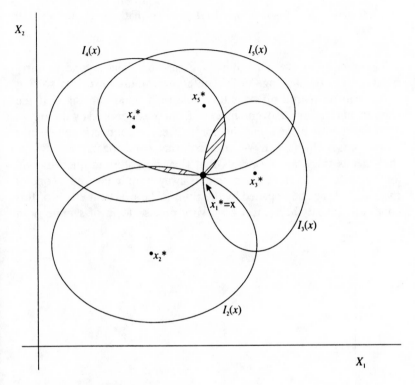

Figure 6.4. Disequilibrium at x

uses a gradient method to explore the local stability of voting procedures.

A. Contract Curves through the Equilibrium

When the number of voters is odd and no two voters have the same ideal point, it turns out that a very demanding symmetry condition is not only sufficient for equilibrium, but is also necessary. For a point x to be an equilibrium, it is necessary and sufficient that the preferences be arranged as follows:

1. x is the ideal point of one voter (meaning $x = x_1^*$ for voter 1), and
2. The remaining voters can be "paired off" so that the contract curve connecting them "goes through" x (it is possible to regroup the

remaining $N - 1$ voters into $\{i, j\}$ pairs so that $x \in C_{ij}$ for all such pairs).

The conditions are illustrated in Figure 6.5. The second requirement is very demanding. Voter preferences must be drawn so that voters can be paired off on either side of x, guaranteeing that the support of one for a movement away from x is opposed by the other. This pairing off means that the contract curve connecting these two voters passes through x. When a contract curve passes through x, that means there are no points that the two voters in question will jointly prefer to x. Hence, movements away from x favored by one of them will always be opposed by the other. The practical effect of this condition is that there must be a very precise form of symmetry in

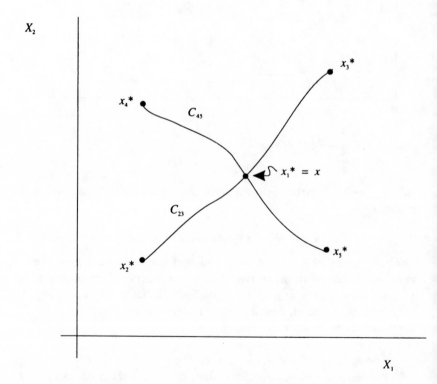

Figure 6.5. Equilibrium at x: Pairing Voters by Contract Curves

the arrangement of the voters' preferences if x is to be an equilibrium.

If the preferences deviate just slightly from the pattern sketched in Figure 6.5, x is no longer an equilibrium. In Figure 6.6, the preferences have been changed just slightly, so that the contract curve connecting voters 2 and 5 no longer passes through x. A majority of voters will favor movement away from x in any of the directions marked by arrows.

B. Illustration of Instability with Circular Preferences

Some very important aspects of the instability of majority rule can be illustrated with figures that represent preferences based solely on distance from the voter's ideal point (see Feld and Grofman, 1987).

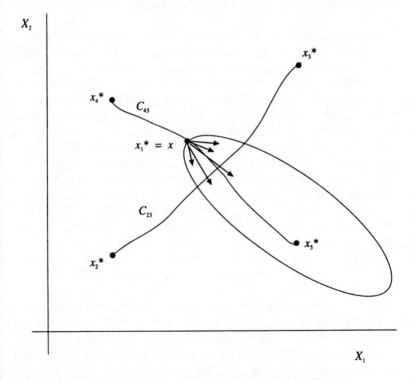

Figure 6.6. Disequilibrium at x: Contract Curves Do Not Cross at x

An alternative x is more attractive than y if it is closer to the ideal point x_i^*. A utility function representation of these preferences uses the "Euclidean norm" to measure the distance between two points, and the utility of any point, such as $x = (x_1, x_2, \ldots, x_m)$, is lower when it is further from the ideal point, $x_i^* = (x_{i1}^*, x_{i2}^*, \ldots, x_{im}^*)$. The formula is

$$U_i(x) = -\left[(x_1 - x_{i1}^*)^2 + \cdots (x_j - x_{ij}^*)^2 + (x_m - x_{im}^*)^2\right]$$

Strictly speaking, if utility is to be proportional to distance, it would be necessary to take the square root of the quantity in parentheses (remember the Pythagorean theorem!). However, since we are dealing with ordinal preferences, any increasing function of U_i is allowed, so certainly the square of the distance represents the same preferences as the distance itself. Either way, the indifference curves are the same.

This model, called the Euclidean model of preferences, is workable for any Euclidean space of dimension m, but the most valuable insights can be found in a two-dimensional model. In a two-dimensional voting problem, the preferred-to sets are "open disks" with the ideal point at the center. The indifference curves are circles centered on the ideal point. Because of this property, the contract curve between any two voters is a straight line. The convex hull of the ideal points forms the Pareto set, the set of points such that there is no way to make one member better off without harming one of the other voters. (The convex hull of a set of points is formed by connecting the points by straight lines and then including all space inside the shape created by the lines.) Five voters with Euclidean preferences are illustrated in Figure 6.7. The Pareto set performs the role for a group of voters that a contract curve performs for a pair of voters. We would never expect the group to settle on a policy outside the Pareto set—they could all be better off by moving into the Pareto set.

An analogy to the median voter theorem can be derived and used to illustrate the instability of majority rule. In the one-dimensional model, the median voter's ideal point was a stable equilibrium because the voters were evenly balanced on either side of it. In a multidimensional model, Davis, Degroot, and Hinich (1972) proved a theorem stating that a point is a majority rule equilibrium only if it is

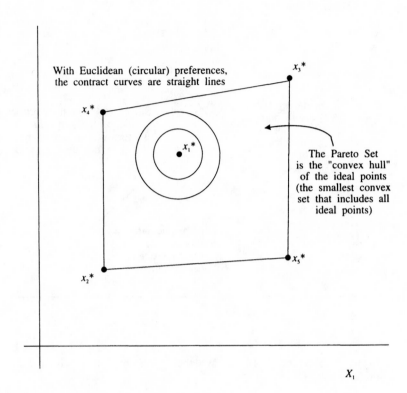

Figure 6.7. Euclidean Preferences

a "median in all directions." If x is an equilibrium, there cannot be a majority of ideal points on one side of a line through x (if the space has more dimensions, a plane through x is used). Otherwise, that majority would vote against x if it were challenged by a point y that is on "their side" of the line. Hence, if x is a median in all directions, then any line through x divides the ideal points evenly.

To illustrate why this must be the case, Enelow and Hinich (1984, pp. 27–29) provide a clear geometrical exposition. The essence of this is illustrated in Figure 6.8. If preferences are circular, a point x will lose the support against a point y that is closer to that voter's ideal point. To find out if y is indeed closer to the ideal point, draw the straight line connecting x and y and mark the midway point on that line. Then draw a line through that midway point that is perpendicu-

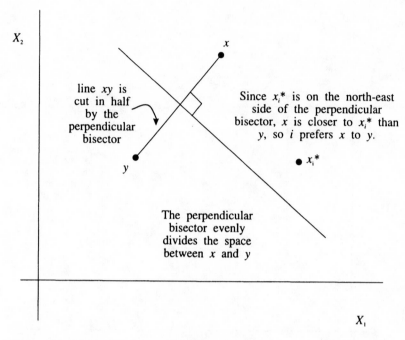

Figure 6.8. Method of Testing Whether i Prefers x to y with Euclidean Preferences

lar to the xy line. This line is called a *perpendicular bisector*. In choosing between x and y, i will favor x if i's ideal point x_i^* is on the same side of the perpendicular bisector as x. If i's ideal point is on the perpendicular bisector, i is indifferent because his ideal point is equidistant from the two points.

Now, considering the point x, we ask, "Is it an equilibrium point?" If it is, it must be that no point y is preferred by a majority. Given the analysis in the previous paragraph, this means that after the perpendicular bisector of the xy line is drawn, there is not a majority of voters on the y side of the line. In Figure 6.9, one will find a five voter example in which x is not an equilibrium point because y is preferred to it. Four of the five voters' ideal points are on the same side of the perpendicular bisector as y.

The next step in the analysis requires a little imagination. Suppose we move the point y closer and closer to x. As we move y closer and

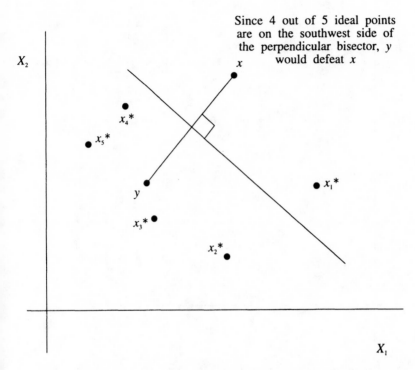

Since 4 out of 5 ideal points are on the southwest side of the perpendicular bisector, y would defeat x

Figure 6.9. Disequilibrium: Testing x with the Perpendicular Bisector

closer to x, the xy line gets shorter and the accompanying perpendicular bisector of the xy line moves closer and closer to x. Eventually, when y gets "arbitrarily close" to x, all we can see is the perpendicular bisector and the bisector is, essentially, a line through x. The point x is stable against a challenge by y only if there is not a majority of the voters' ideal points on the y side of the line.

The proposed equilibrium point x must be majority-preferred to alternatives in any direction. As shown in Figure 6.10, a point x must be stable not only against y, but also against movement in the opposite direction of y. Hence, the observation that there must not be a majority on the y side of the line implies there must not be a majority on the opposite side either. If there is no majority on either side, the line through x is a "median line." A "median in all directions" is a point x such that no line through x leaves a majority

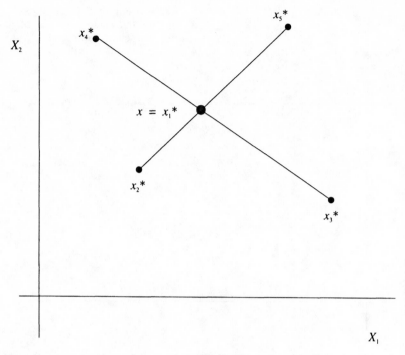

X_2

x_4^*

x_5^*

$x = x_1^*$

x_2^*

x_3^*

X_1

Figure 6.10. Equilibrium: Policy x is a Median in all Directions

on either side of the line. In that sense, Davis, DeGroot, and Hinich found that x can be a majority rule equilibrium only if it is a median in all directions. A five voter example with Euclidean preferences is illustrated in Figure 6.10. Note the "median lines" serve the same function as contract curves in the more general model.

*C. Utility Gradient Conditions

The final approach to stability of a multidimensional model requires multivariate calculus, so some readers may prefer to skip this section. This section is worth studying because the approach allows for additional insights and generalizations beyond majority rule decision-making (McKelvey and Schofield, 1987).

For an m-dimensional space, the utility function is $U_i(x) = U_i(x_1, x_2, \ldots, x_m)$. If we assume this function is differentiable everywhere, then the **gradient** of U_i exists (symbolized ∇U_i). The gradient is a vector of first partial derivatives of U_i:

$$\nabla U_i(x) = (\partial U_i / \partial x_1, \partial U_i / \partial x_2, \ldots, \partial U_i / \partial x_m)$$

The gradient has some very interesting properties, which are illustrated in a two-dimensional model in Figure 6.11. The gradient $\nabla U_i(x)$ at a point $x = (x_1, x_2)$ is seen as a vector beginning at x and pointing away from it. If the gradient $\nabla U_i(x_1, x_2)$ is (1, 2), for example, that means the gradient is a vector which begins at $x = (x_1, x_2)$ and ends at $(x_1 + 1, x_2 + 2)$. The gradient is perpendicular (at a right angle) to the indifference curve $I_i(x)$.

The gradient points in the direction of greatest increase in utility. Of course, any small move in a direction pointing into the convex set $P_i(x)$ will have i's support. The movement cannot be too great,

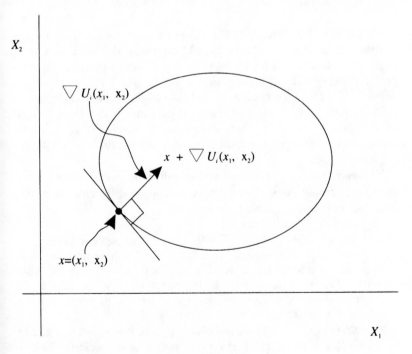

Figure 6.11. Gradient Analysis of Preferences

however, because it might "overshoot" the preferred-to set by hopping over $P_i(x)$. The direction of a move toward point $y = (y_1, y_2)$ from x is formally represented as the difference between x and the destination point:

$$v_y = (y - x) = (y_1 - x_1, y_2 - x_2)$$

Hence, the point y can be viewed as x plus a move in the direction of y, or $y = x + v_y$.

If we want to know if a voter will prefer a move in the direction of y, we can use the concept of the inner product. The inner product of two vectors, for example, (a, b) and (d, e), is defined as $(ad + be)$. Multiply the jth term of the vectors together and sum the results. The inner product $\nabla U_i \cdot v_y$ can be used to indicate if the move in the direction of y is desirable to i. An inner product is defined as

$$\nabla U_i(x) \cdot v_y = \partial U_i / \partial x_1 \cdot (y_1 - x_1) + \partial U_i / \partial x_2 \cdot (y_2 - x_2)$$

We know from elementary linear algebra that if the inner product is 0, then ∇U_i and v_y are "orthogonal," meaning they are at a right angle to each other. If so, then the vector v_y is not pointing into the preferred-to set. If the inner product is negative, it means the angle between ∇U_i and v_y is obtuse. The obtuse angle means that v_y is not pointing into $P_i(x)$. A positive inner product means the angle formed by ∇U_i and v_y is acute. This is the case in which the voter would favor a move away from x toward y, since the vector points into the preferred-to set.

Slutsky (1979, p. 1117) showed the following holds when preferences are strictly convex and represented by a differentiable utility function. For any direction $v_y = (y - x)$:

1. If $\nabla U_i(x) \cdot v_y \leq 0$, then $U_i(x) > U_i(x + v_y)$. This means $U_i(x) > U_i(y)$. The inner product indicates that either v_y is orthogonal to or at an obtuse angle with $\nabla U_i(x)$. Hence, v_y is pointing out of the preferred-to set $P_i(x)$. Since movements in the direction of y aim outside the preferred-to set, it does not matter how far one proposed to move. Change in y's direction will be opposed.

2. If $\nabla U_i(x) \cdot v_y > 0$, then there exists a λ^* such that for all $0 < \lambda < \lambda^*$, then $U_i(x + \lambda v_y) > U_i(x)$. The λ is a "scaling factor" indicating how far one can go in the direction of y and still be in $P_i(x)$. The "boundary

number" λ^* is just a bit too far because $x + \lambda^* v_y$ is in $I_i(x)$, but any λ less than λ^* will do. If the inner product is positive, we are certain that by putting λ equal to a small number, say 0.01, that the point $x + 0.01 v_y$ is preferred to x. If 0.01 is too large, some smaller number will suffice. Perhaps most importantly, we know that if the gradient is positive, then we can make λ very small—get "arbitrarily close" to x—and $x + \lambda y$ will be preferred to x. This will be true for all directions that point into $P_i(x)$, even if they are almost perpendicular to the gradient.

How does this analysis of utility gradients help us to characterize a majority rule equilibrium? Suppose we have an odd number of voters and that one voter has an ideal point at the equilibrium point x. If the voters consider moving just a little bit in the direction of a point y, the voters for whom $\nabla U_i \cdot v_y > 0$ will vote in favor. To guarantee that the movement toward y will be defeated, it must be that at least one-half of the voters are opposed:

$$|\{i \in N: \nabla U_i \cdot v_y \leq 0\}| \geq N/2$$

or equivalently

$$|\{i \in N: \nabla U_i \cdot v_y > 0\}| < N/2$$

Considering a movement toward y, there must be at least $N/2$ voters whose utility gradients are orthogonal to or at an obtuse angle with v_y. This condition must hold in each possible direction of movement, a fact which implies the very well known "radial symmetry" condition discovered in a pioneering paper by Plott (1967). As illustrated in the Figure 6.12, if no two voters have the same ideal point and N is odd, x can be a majority equilibrium only if:

1. there is one voter for whom $\nabla U_i(x) = 0$ (meaning x is that voter's ideal point), and
2. there is a way to partition the voters into pairs in which their utility gradients point in opposite directions.

The method of formalizing the notion of gradients in the opposite directions is this: it is possible to partition the voters into $\{i, j\}$ pairs such that

$$\nabla U_i(x) = -\lambda \cdot \nabla U_j(d) \quad \text{for some } \lambda > 0$$

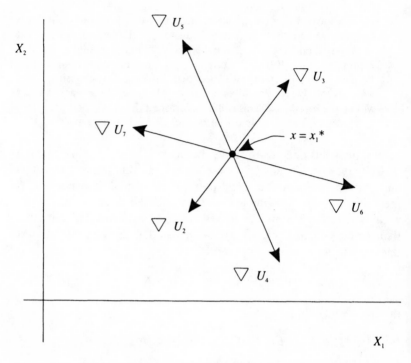

Figure 6.12. Gradient Symmetry Condition for Majority Rule Equilibrium at Policy x

If such a value for λ exists, then it means that the gradients of i and j point in opposite directions.

A slight deviation from these conditions will guarantee that x is no longer an equilibrium point (for a consideration of the complications that arise when N is even or when some voters have identical ideal points, see Enelow and Hinich, 1983a).

The three treatments of majority rule in multidimensional space lead to slight different insights, but the major conclusion is the same: Majority rule equilibrium exists under very stringent conditions. It is important for the reader to see that the stability analyses of parts A, B, and C are closely interrelated. The gradient approach allows us to focus on the local stability properties of majority rule equilibrium, whereas the others offer global stability properties. What we have found is that unless each voter's tendency to vote in directions away from x is exactly matched by an opposing voter's tendency, then x cannot be an equilibrium. The pairing of voters through connecting contract curves is precisely the same as the pairing of gradients, since the gradients point in opposite directions *along the contract curve.* The median in all directions argument implies that there is never a majority of ideal points on one side of that contract curve. How can we be sure that no such majority exists? When preferences are circular, the contract curves are straight lines. We must arrange the voters' ideal points in a "radially symmetric" pattern, so that they are paired with the contract curve between them going through x. The intersecting contract curve result in part A means that the ideal points (of voters with circular preferences) can be paired off and connected by straight lines and all of the lines intersect at the equilibrium. If such a condition is satisfied, the "contract lines" divide the ideal points so that there is never a majority of ideal points on one side of any line, precisely the "median in all directions" requirement. It is easy to see that the median in all directions requirement imposed with circular preferences implies that the gradients are paired in opposite directions. With circular preferences, the gradient at x points at a voter's ideal point, and hence drawing preferences with opposing gradients is equivalent to drawing a straight contract line connecting the two voters' ideal points.

The Chaos Theorems

If there is no equilibrium point, what then? Perhaps there is a small top-cycle set X^{top} to which majority rule outcomes are confined (Tullock, 1967). At worst, intuition tells us that majority rule outcomes will be inside the Pareto set. Sadly, these optimistic interpretations are not correct. In a very influential article, McKelvey (1976, p. 475) showed that "when transitivity breaks down, it *completely* breaks down, engulfing the whole space in a single cycle set." This was the first of many "chaos theorems" that have appeared in the literature. McKelvey's major result is a theorem stating that when there is no equilibrium point, then one can find an agenda leading from *any* alternative x to *any* other alternative y. The agenda is a sequence of alternatives $\{x, z^1, z^2, \ldots, z^k, y\}$, such that z^1 defeats x, z^2 defeats z^1, z^3 defeats z^2, and so on until z^k defeats z^{k-1} and y knocks off z^k.

78

With Euclidean (or circular) preferences, this claim is very easy to illustrate. The key is to design an agenda that swings far away from x to some point z^k. From there, the voters can be (unanimously) induced to favor y over z^k. In Figure 6.13 there is an example of three voters with circular preferences. The contract curves $C_{12} C_{23} C_{13}$ form the outer edges of the Pareto set, which is a triangle. There is no majority rule equilibrium because all three ideal points do not lie on a straight line, an illustration of the symmetry condition for equilibrium that was outlined above. The figure shows an agenda—a series of proposals, z^1, z^2, z^3, z^4—that leads away from the initial point x. The point z^1 defeats x because it is closer to the contract curve (and hence the ideal points) of voters 1 and 2. Voter 3 is unhappy with the move to z^1, but the others are a majority and there is nothing 3 can do about it. The agenda continues, however, and 3

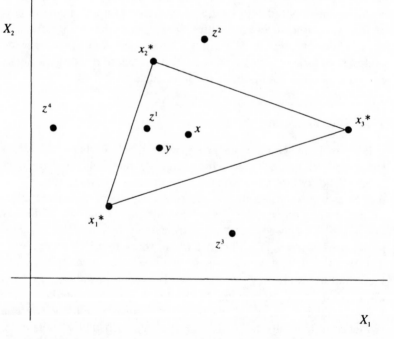

Figure 6.13. Agenda z^1, z^2, z^3, z^4 Leading away from x. Outside the Pareto Set, and back to y

sees a chance to improve his position. The point z^2 is better for voter 3 and it will also be preferred by 2. By hopping in this fashion, the agenda can go as far from x as we would like, and *each step is preferred by a majority!* The most puzzling and troublesome fact about this voting agenda is that majority rule can lead *outside the Pareto set.* After we have hopped far enough outside the Pareto set, we can offer the voters policy y, which they unanimously prefer.

Recently, using advanced methods from topology, a number of articles have addressed additional questions about the existence and stability of equilibrium. Without going into details, a sketch of the highlights can be presented. Consider, $\mathcal{U}^N$, the set of all possible social utility profiles in which each voter's preferences are quasi-concave. Refer to the subset of profiles for which there is an equilibrium point as M^*. To what extent does M^* fill up $\mathcal{U}^N$? "Hardly at all," is the nontechnical version of the answer. This is true in the sense that the set of equilibrium-inducing profiles is "nowhere dense." Nowhere denseness means that one can pick any profile, $U \in M^*$, and change it in the slightest possible way to create a new profile, say V, for which there is no equilibrium point (Schofield, 1980; Cox, 1987a). By analogy, consider a dart board in which the background coloring represents the "no equilibrium" profiles and razor thin lines dividing the colored sections represent profiles that have equilibrium points. If a dart is thrown at the board, what is the probability that it will hit a razor thin line? Somewhere between slim and none. What is the probability that it will land in a colored area? One, or some number very close to it.

Norman Schofield has been a leading scholar in this field, and two of his most important contributions lie in this line of study. Consider the space of all possible social preference profiles that are "smooth," meaning that they are continuous and that their slopes change gradually (technically, they can be differentiated repeatedly). If the dimension of the choice space is "high enough" (greater than a constant called the Nakamura number), Schofield (1983) shows that there is no majority rule equilibrium point for "almost all" smooth profiles. With an odd number of voters, the instability exists if there are two or more dimensions, while for an even number of voters, three or more dimensions are required. A definition of "high enough" using the so-called Nakamura number can be applied to any kind of "simple" voting procedure, one in which the voters can be divided into a winning and losing coalitions. Furthermore, although

McKelvey's theorem on global cycles is illustrated with hops to and from distant points in the policy space, Schofield showed that these hops are not necessary in order for a cycle to exist. The utility gradient model discussed above implied that if a point can be defeated, it can be defeated by points very close to it in the space. Hence, majority rule can meander around in a smooth cycle (a continuous connected curve with no hops) if there is no equilibrium point. Schofield (1978a, 1980, 1983) showed that "almost all" points in a policy space of sufficiently high dimension can be contained in a smooth cycle if there is no majority rule equilibrium. For majority rule in two dimensions with an odd number of voters, the smooth cycle can go virtually anywhere inside the Pareto set, but not outside. For higher dimensions, the smooth cycle can go outside the Pareto set.

Addressing the Disequilibrium Problem

People disagree about the meaning of the possibility of "global cycles." Some scholars emphasize the fundamental instability of majority rule and raise the possibility that social systems may be cycling. Schofield (1978b, p. 3) once commented, "To the observation that pluralist societies are in fact stable, one could reply that the only logical inference is that the decision procedure must be collegial or oligarchic. I prefer to suppose that pluralist societies are in fact potentially unstable, but that from our local perspective we are unaware of the phenomena of cycles. Indeed I find the conclusion that political behavior (and for that matter economic behavior) is indeterminate rather satisfying."

Some examples of instability in actual majority rule decision-making have been discovered. Nevertheless, the claim that policy is perpetually cycling is difficult to accept. Laws stay on the books for years. The most prevalent observation about the U.S. Congress seems to be that change is very difficult to implement. The apparent stability of policy is a stark contrast to the instability prevalent in the theory. This contrast caused Tullock (1981) to ask the now famous question, "Why so much stability?" in an essay that kicked-off a symposium in *Public Choice*.

One solution that has been considered is that the voters could "trade votes" to achieve a mutually beneficial outcome. Unless special procedures are created to enforce agreements among legislators, a system with vote trading is as unstable as pure majority rule. Readers are encouraged to consult Schwartz's (1977, 1981, 1986) research on this problem. Schwartz showed that if majority rule is unstable, then any outcome that might be arrived at by vote trading can be overturned by another proposed vote trade. This result caused some to consider the possibility that instead of trading votes, members ought to be allowed to exchange *cash* to influence each other's votes (Tullock, 1992). Aside from the obvious ethical problem, it appears that this approach would not eliminate the danger of cycles (Pun, 1997).

Aside from vote trading, there are two major approaches to explain the apparent stability of public policy. The first approach adds structure—additional procedures and rules—that guides policy toward a "structure-induced equilibrium," an idea introduced by Shepsle (1979). The second approach is to alter the assumptions about the behavior of political actors to make them either more sophisticated and informed or significantly less well informed.

Structure-Induced Equilibrium

The structure-induced equilibrium is aptly named. Stability of legislative policy results from the addition of institutional and procedural details. Observing that the model that leads to the chaos theorems is "highly atomistic and institutionally sparse," Shepsle (1979, p. 27) introduced the notion of structure-induced equilibrium. Shepsle observed that participants in "real life" legislatures are restricted by parliamentary procedures that limit amendments and organize voting procedures. In legislatures, majorities are not allowed to wander in any direction. The so-called new institutionalism in political science combines the methods of rational choice analysis with models of these legislative procedures and institutional details (see McCubbins and Sullivan, 1987).

A variety of institutions have been examined. One of the most important sources of stability in the U.S. Congress might be the rules that govern the order of voting, the agenda. When a bill is proposed, amendments are considered in a particular way, and at the end of the consideration process, the status quo is always compared against the "perfected" (meaning amended if necessary) alternative. This means that, in the end, only policies that are majority-preferred to the status quo may be adopted.

The size of the required majority also has a significant stabilizing effect. So far, pure majority rule—50% + 1—has been explored in this book. What if the rules require that more than 60%, or two-thirds, or even three-quarters of the members agree before a policy can defeat the status quo. This requirement is sometimes called superma-jority rule or α-majority rule. An α-majority rule is one that requires that a proportion of the voters more than α must favor y in order for it to defeat x. Early research on the stability of the α-majority rule inspired the "gradient symmetry conditions" that were discussed above (Slutsky, 1979; Greenberg, 1979; see also McKelvey and Schofield, 1987, for gradient conditions that apply to more proce-dures). It is obvious that, if $\alpha = 1$, then there can be no cycles. A requirement of unanimity means that the status quo can be defeated only if everyone agrees. A requirement of unanimity—or very near unanimity—has been proposed by some authors, the most notable being Buchanan and Tullock (1962). Unanimity has the unfortunate consequence, however, that it can "freeze-in" policies that are widely disliked, but cannot be changed because they benefit a small minor-ity. So the question becomes, if we desire policies that are stable and yet meaningfully reflective of the will of the majority, how small should we make α? Ingenious research by Caplin and Nalebuff (1988, 1991) has shown that if α is about 64%, then α-majority rule in a multidimensional space has an equilibrium point. This result, which applies to a relatively broad spectrum of utility functions and distributions of voter ideal points, guarantees that the mean (and possibly points around it) is stable in α-majority voting. Furthermore, the mean is in the center of the distribution of ideal points, so moderate policy results are stable.

The most common subject of study for the structure-induced equilibrium proponents has been the legislature. Shepsle's (1979) original essay on the subject presents a rich model of Congressional committees and their jurisdictions. Stability is induced by breaking the multidimensional space into many one-dimensional spaces. If a committee has control over only a single dimension, then we should expect the median of committee members' ideal points to be adopted. This basic insight has fueled a large number of studies in which the policy process is viewed as a sequence of one-dimensional decisions, possibly involving a committee, the whole Congress, the president, an administrative agency, or the judiciary. If committee members have a "veto power" on proposals, they can block policy changes that the whole legislature might adopt. An interested reader ought to consult the highly influential essay by Weingast and Marshall (1988), which interprets congressional institutions as mechanisms that stabilize legislative decision-making and enforce agreements among individual legislators (see also Denzau and Mackay, 1983). There is now a large literature on the question of whether committee members are preference "outliers," atypical of the rest of the legislature, with a tendency to draw policy outcomes to the extremes (Gilligan and Krehbiel, 1987; Krehbiel, 1991, 1997; Groseclose, 1994; Dion and Huber, 1996).

To illustrate the stabilizing effect of procedures and institutions, consider the following in-depth examples.

Example 6.1. Issue-at-a-Time Voting

Shepsle and Weingast (1981) gave a simple example of an equilibrium point induced by the requirement that issues are considered one at a time (see also Kadane, 1972). Some legislative procedures require the legislators to select a policy on one dimension before they consider the next dimension. Any member can introduce an amendment—a change from one point in the space to another—as long as the amendment changes only one dimension at a time. Rules in the U.S. House of Representatives, for example, require that all amendments be "germane," meaning relevant to the policy being debated. In a two-dimensional space, this means that amendments can move horizontally or vertically, but not diagonally.

Most of the basic research on issue-at-a-time voting has been done with preferences that are represented by the weighted Euclidean distance (WED) model, a classic tool in social choice theory (Davis and Hinich, 1966, 1967; see also Davis, Hinich, and Ordeshook, 1970). This is a classic and widely used model with which students ought to be familiar. The WED model is a utility function that assigns numerical utility to each possible policy. The voter is made more and more unhappy as policy moves away from the ideal point. The amount of the unhappiness is measured by the distance of the movement away from the voter's ideal.

As illustrated in the two-dimensional model in Figure 6.14, the indifference curves of the WED model are always circles or ovals.

a) Circular Preferences:

$a_{11} = a_{22}, \quad a_{12} = 0$

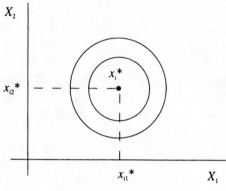

b) Separable Preferences:

$a_{11} \neq a_{22}, \ a_{12} = 0$

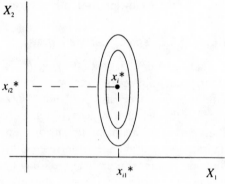

c) Noncircular, Nonseparable Preferences:

$a_{11} \neq a_{22}, \ a_{12} \neq 0$

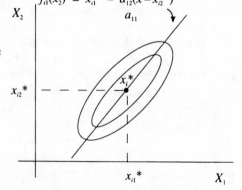

Figure 6.14. Weighted Euclidean Distance

The voter i's ideal point is $x_i^* = (x_{i1}^*, x_{i2}^*)$. Recall the first subscript refers to the voter, the second to the dimension. Movements away from x_i^* to a point $x = (x_1, x_2)$ cause utility to decline "quadratically," as represented by the expression

$$U_i(x) = a_{11}(x_1 - x_{i1}^*)^2 + 2a_{12}(x_1 - x_{i1}^*)(x_2 - x_{i2}^*) + a_{22}(x_2 - x_{i2}^*)^2$$

The weighting coefficients a_{11}, a_{12}, and a_{22} are restricted to assure that utility declines as x moves away from x_i^*, so $a_{11} < 0$, $a_{22} < 0$, and $a_{11}a_{22} - a_{12}^2 > 0$. The coefficients a_{11}, a_{22}, and a_{12} determine the shape of the voter indifference curves. Coefficient a_{11} indicates how sensitive overall utility is to a change in the first dimension of public policy, and a_{22} indicates the same for the second dimension. Coefficient a_{12} indicates the extent of the interaction between dimensions 1 and 2 in the opinion of the voter. If that coefficient is not zero, then the desirability of changes in one dimension can depend on the other dimension. This coefficient determines whether preferences on the various dimensions are separable or not.

Voters' preferences are said to be **separable** if the favorite policy on one dimension does not depend on the position that is adopted on the other dimension. Does your position on funding for Medicare depend on the number of U.S. troops in Bosnia? If not, your preferences are separable. The coefficient a_{12} is an indicator of the separability of the two issues. If $a_{11} = a_{22}$ and $a_{12} = 0$, the indifference curves are circular (as noted above, this is called the Euclidean model of preferences). Many examples in the social choice literature use Euclidean preferences. If $a_{11} \neq a_{22}$ and $a_{12} = 0$, preferences are still separable, but the indifference curves become ovals, stretched vertically or horizontally, but always parallel to the axes. If $a_{12} \neq 0$, then preferences are not separable. That means that if the society chooses a position on the first dimension that differs from a voter's ideal, then that voter should be expected to adjust (or recalculate) his/her stance on the second dimension to suit the result from the first.

We will first consider issue-by-issue voting with separable preferences. We think of the legislature as voters $i = 1, \ldots, N$. Policy begins at some point in the space, say $x = (x_1, x_2)$. An amendment is a proposed change in one dimension. Suppose a legislature first considers policy X_1. Afterward, the second policy is considered, knowing the decision on the first dimension. A five voter legislature is illustrated in Figure 6.15. The ideal points on the first dimension are marked below the X_1 axis in this order $\{x_{11}^*, x_{21}^*, x_{31}^*, x_{41}^*, x_{51}^*\}$. Proposals are allowed only if they move horizontally. Readers will recall the median voter theorem, which implies that the median of the ideal points, x_3^*, is an equilibrium decision on the first dimension. Considering a selection from X_2, the most-preferred values are, from bottom to top, $\{x_{12}^*, x_{22}^*, x_{52}^*, x_{42}^*, x_{32}^*\}$. We can see that voter 5's most preferred setting for dimension 2, x_{52}^*, will be chosen because it is the median of the ideal points. Hence, the majority rule equilibrium (x_{31}^*, x_{52}^*) is the median of the issues considered separately. One difference from the institution-free multidimensional model is appar-

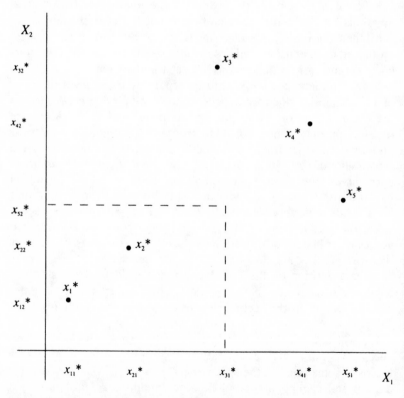

Figure 6.15. Equilibrium Induced by Division of the Question

ent. The equilibrium need not be the ideal point of any particular voter.

There is one particularly appealing property of issue-by-issue voting with separable preferences. It doesn't matter whether the legislature considers issue dimension X_1 or X_2 first. The winning proposal on dimension 2 is always the median ideal point, and this is unaffected by the decision the voters have already made on dimension 1. It does not matter whether they expect to have a chance to go back and vote on the first dimension again.

This pleasant property does not hold up when voter preferences are nonseparable. In our first pass at issue-by-issue voting when preferences are not separable, we will assume that voters are *myopic*. While voting on dimension 1, they take the status quo policy choice on the second dimension as a "given." They do not have "foresight" to vote on dimension 1 in anticipation of the changes they may make on dimension 2 when it is considered.

Recall that nonseparable preferences exist if $a_{12} \neq 0$. In that case, the most preferred value of x_1 will depend on the selection of x_2. The optimal choice of x_1 is given by this function, which depends on x_2 (see Enelow and Hinich, 1984a, p. 19):

$$f_{i1}(x_2) = x_{i1}^* - (a_{12}/a_{11})(x_2 - x_{i2}^*)$$

The tricky thing about evaluating issue-by-issue voting is that the current policy on X_2 will influence each voter's decision about X_1. If x_2^0 is the status quo on X_2 and the voters act as if x_2^0 will continue to be social policy after X_1 is considered, then the majority rule winner on dimension 1 will be the median of this set of points: $\{f_{11}(x_2^0), f_{21}(x_2^0), f_{31}(x_2^0), f_{41}(x_2^0), f_{51}(x_2^0)\}$. The succinct notation for this is $\{f_{i1}(x_1^0)\}_{i \in N}$, meaning a set of points, one for each $i \in N$. Let the median of this set be equal to x_1^0. After this dimension is determined, the voters will turn to consider X_2. Suppose that, after observing x_1^0, the most preferred levels on dimension 2 are $\{f_{12}(x_1^0), f_{22}(x_1^0), f_{32}(x_1^0), f_{42}(x_1^0), f_{52}(x_1^0)\}$. The median of these points, called x_2^1 will be the winner. That median point of a set is sometimes referred to as

$$\text{med}\{f_{i2}(x_1^0)\}_{i \in N}$$

This is the stage of analysis at which nonseparable preferences cause a major problem. After the voters have settled on policy x_2^1, one of them might propose that they reopen their decision on X_1. If they do, the induced most-preferred points of voters $i = 1-5$, $\{f_{i1}(x_2^1)\}_{i \in N}$, will differ from the most-preferred points that assumed the decision on X_2 would be x_2^0. Hence, it is virtually certain a new choice x_1^1 will be arrived at. We could imagine a sequence of decisions on the issues in which the legislature mindlessly decides dimension 1, then dimension 2, then dimension 1, etc.

The sequential adjustment process can be illustrated graphically (see Black and Newing, 1951; Shepsle, 1979, p. 48; Denzau and Mackay, 1981, p. 769). The first step is to make calculations about what each voter will prefer on each dimension, given a decision on the other dimension. Such analysis for dimension 1 is illustrated in Figure 6.16. The lines f_{11}, f_{12}, f_{13}, f_{14}, and f_{15} represent the induced most-preferred points on dimension 1 for the five voters. For each point on the second dimension, these lines indicate the most desirable setting for policy in the first dimension. The emphasized parts of these lines in the figure make up the median voter "ridge line," which we refer to as $M_1(x_2)$. As x_2 ranges from low to high, the voter preferences for the first dimension change, and the median of their preferences changes as well. The ridge line tracks that median. This line is formally defined for each value of x_2 as

$$M_1(x_2) = \{(x_1, x_2) \mid x_1 = \text{med}\{f_{i1}(x_2)\}_{i \in N} \text{ and } x_2 \in X_2\}$$

For any given x_2, the majority rule winner on X_1 will be on this ridge line because the ridge line tracks the induced most-preferred point of the median voter. One fact that people find surprising is that as x_2 varies from low to high, the identity of the median voter on dimension 1 changes. In Figure 6.16, the median voter is voter 2 for the lowest values of x_2, and as x_2 is increased, the median voter becomes voter number 4, then voter 3.

It is possible to develop a median voter ridge line to illustrate the median preference on dimension 2 as a function of choices on dimension 1. The issue-by-issue equilibrium is the point where the two ridge lines cross. Shepsle (1979) showed that an equilibrium always exists. In Figure 6.17, a sequence of issue-by-issue votes will converge to the equilibrium, as indicated by the sequence of arrows indicating what will happen in a voting process beginning at the point (x_1^0, x_2^0).

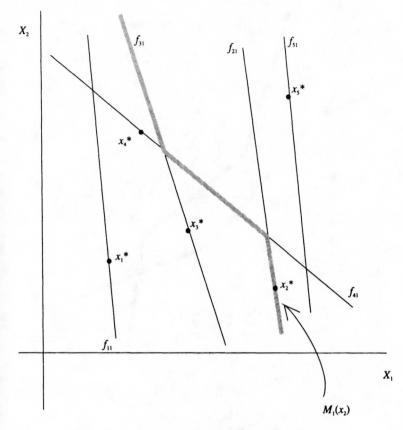

For each possible choice along the
vertical axis, the f_{i1} curves indicate the
most preferred level on the horizontal
axis for each voter, $i=1,...,5$. The ridge line $M_1(x_2)$
traces the position of the median voter
on X_1 for each value of x_2.

Figure 6.16. Derivation of a Ridge Line

It is not always true that issue-by-issue voting will "home in" on
the equilibrium point, however. The convergence of the voting process depends on the slopes of the median ridge lines. It is possible to
sketch voter preferences that cause issue-by-issue voting to diverge
away from the equilibrium.

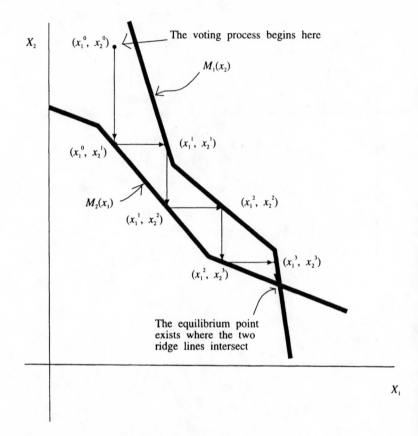

Figure 6.17. Issue-at-a-Time Majority Rule

The possibility of nonconvergence is not a new idea at this stage of our analysis—the analysis of the multidimensional model is based on the idea of disequilibrium. However, the problem takes on a new quality here because an equilibrium point does exist, but it is not selected. One research strategy is to consider voter foresight. The model that we have been discussing has treated voters as very naive actors who are only capable of after-the-fact adjustment. The model treats voters as myopic actors, who have no ability to anticipate the effect of current decisions on future decisions. Instead, a better approach might be to redesign the way that voters forecast future decisions and adjust their behavior in early stages of the voting agenda. In the studies by Denzau and Mackay (1981), Enelow and Hinich (1983b, 1984b), and Epple and Kadane (1990), this has been the strategy. Even in those more complicated models, voting procedures might not converge to an equilibrium point.

The upshot of the many studies on issue-at-a-time voting is that the restriction of proposals to horizontal and vertical movements can have a significant stabilizing effect on social choice. Under some conditions, that restriction alone is enough to induce stability in multidimensional voting. When preferences are not separable, however, and drawn "just so," it is possible to find that, even though an equilibrium exists, majority rule may wander away from it. When that is the case, it seems likely that other institutional procedures, such as rules governing the agenda, come into play. Typically, legislative leaders will try to guide the members to consider one dimension to its completion, and then move on.

Example 6.2. A Bicameral System

Hammond and Miller (1987) proposed a model to represent decision-making in a bicameral legislature. A status quo point is given, and it remains in effect until a change is agreed to by majorities in two houses of the legislature. In the United States, for example, a policy change must pass both the House and the Senate. Hammond and Miller show that even though there is no majority rule equilibrium in either house, or when voters from both houses are combined in a single legislature, there may be equilibrium points in a bicameral legislature. (Note: Hammond and Miller use the game theoretic term "core" and develop some differences between that concept and equilibrium. In this particular example, the core is the same as the equilibrium, so we continue to use the term equilibrium for continuity. In their terminology, a point x is in the core if there is no coalition with the authority to implement change that prefers to do so. This point is quite naturally referred to as an equilibrium.)

Consider Figure 6.18, which is an adaptation of Hammond and Miller's Figure 1 (1987, p. 1158). The policy space is two dimensional and the voters are assumed to have circular (Euclidean) preferences. The voters are named by their ideal points, $h_1^*, h_2^*, h_3^*, s_1^*, s_2^*, s_3^*$. If

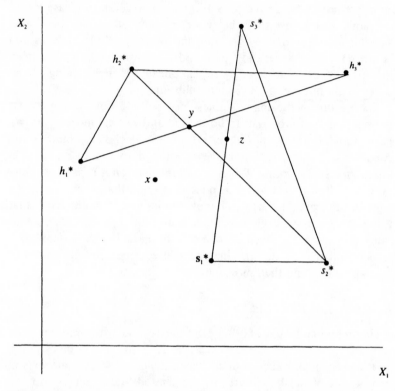

Figure 6.18. Bicameral Legislature with Structure-Induced Equilibrium

we treat these legislators as a six-person group, a majority is four members. According to the median-in-all-directions result discussed above, if x is to be an equilibrium point, there must be no more than three voters on one side of any line drawn through x. Obviously, the condition is not satisfied. Hence, x is not an equilibrium and voting cycles are possible. A little checking should convince the reader that there is no equilibrium point.

Suppose that the members of the House of Representatives have ideal points h_1^*, h_2^*, h_3^*, and the ideal points of the members of the Senate are s_1^*, s_2^*, s_3^*. Majority rule is used within each house to decide if a point can be defeated. The reader can see that a point such as x can be defeated in both houses, but a point such as z cannot. This is a bicameral equilibrium because there is no "joint majority" preferring any point. As an adaptation of the unicameral median-in-all-directions result, Hammond and Miller show that a point z is a bicameral equilibrium point if there is no line through z that leaves a majority of ideal points on one side of the line in each of the chambers.

Behavioral Sources of Stability

Some scholars have argued that the rush to study structures and institutions was misplaced. Instead, they argue, the objective should be to find the "institution-free" properties of social choice. By far, the most widely investigated institution-free solution is the "uncovered set," which was introduced by Miller (1980) and has been refined and extended (for example, Shepsle and Weingast, 1984; Banks, 1985; McKelvey, 1986; Cox, 1987a; Feld, Grofman, and Miller, 1989; Miller, 1995). The uncovered set includes the equilibrium point, if it exists, but the uncovered set exists even if there is no equilibrium. The uncovered set, its proponents argue, is a relatively small set near the geometric center of voter ideal points. If one is convinced that the uncovered set is indeed a normatively desirable solution, the next problem is to find a voting procedure that leads to outcomes in the uncovered set.

The uncovered set is defined in terms of the covering relation. Cox's (1987a, p. 412) definition is this: "x covers y if x is majority-preferred to y and if everything that is majority-preferred to x is also majority preferred to y." A point x would have an irresistible appeal, since it can beat y and any policy that can defeat x would defeat y as well. The uncovered set is, of course, the set of points that are not covered. How could we describe points in the uncovered set? Note the definition has two parts. A point y could be uncovered if (1) there is no x that is majority-preferred to y or (2) some x is majority-preferred to y, *but* there is a point z that y can defeat in a vote and x cannot. The main idea is that a point should be acceptable as a "solution" if it can defeat every other alternative head-on or if the alternatives that can defeat it would in turn be defeated by other alternatives that it can defeat. McKelvey (1986) offered a forceful statement of the idea that the uncovered set is a normatively appealing solution because it is likely to be a small set in the interior of the policy space. As such, the uncovered set has the properties that we were looking for when we investigated the top-cycle set.

The $100,000 question is this: under what conditions will voting processes lead to outcomes that are in the uncovered set? Models of legislative decision-making have been built that argue that when voters are sophisticated and the agenda is fixed, then voting will lead to outcomes that are uncovered. Readers will recall that, in the model of multidimensional chaos, the voters were rather myopic, simply offering their sincere judgments between any two alternatives that were offered up by an agenda-setter. Suppose instead the model postulates **sophisticated voters**, voters who can look ahead into the agenda to see where it is leading them and vote strategically (not revealing their actual preference between alternatives) to affect the eventual outcome. Sophisticated voters need not only information about the agenda, but also detailed knowledge of the preferences of the other voters in order to forecast the eventual social choice. They can anticipate what the majority rule decision will be on the last vote, and then reason backward to conclude what will happen on the second-to-last vote, and so forth. This method of analysis, first proposed Farquharson (1969) and Kramer (1972), was formalized by McKelvey and Niemi (1978). It uses tools from game theory and treats voters as competitors, rather than simple containers (or revealers) of preferences. Miller (1980) and Shepsle and Weingast (1984) showed that sophisticated voting on a fixed agenda typically ends up with outcomes in the uncovered set.

McKelvey's (1986, p. 284) influential article argued that "the uncovered set contains, as subsets, the solutions that arise as game theoretic equilibria in several different institutional settings." He showed, for example, that an "amendment agenda"—one in which two proposals are compared and the winner advances to confront the next in the list—leads into the uncovered set. The force of this argument, however, was weakened significantly by the counterargument made by Ordeshook and Schwartz (1987). When legislative leaders are allowed to design other kinds of agendas, sophisticated voting can lead to outcomes outside the uncovered set. As they argue, "if we properly extend a setter's strategies to include all agendas that we might actually observe in a legislature, strategic voting is not the constraint it was thought to be" (Ordeshook and Schwartz, 1987, p. 188).

While the predictive power of the uncovered set in a legislative setting is debatable, it is still a valuable and important tool in the study of position-taking by political candidates. Suppose that voters who have quasi-concave preferences will choose by majority rule between the policy offerings of two candidates. Suppose candidates know the preferences of the voters, but they must announce their policy proposals simultaneously to the electorate. They have to take stands without knowing the proposal of the other candidate. What stand should a candidate take under those conditions? A wise candidate will choose a position in the uncovered set. As Cox (1987a, p. 420) observed, "If one accepts the extremely mild assumption that candidates will not adopt a spatial strategy y if there is another available strategy x which is at least as good as y against any strategy the opponent might take and is better against some of the opponent's possible strategies, then one can conclude that candidates will confine themselves to strategies in the uncovered set." Cycles are possible, as we know, but they are not observed in an election setting because the candidates are offered just one opportunity to announce their positions.

As a solution strategy, one might argue that the uncovered set imposes too many demands on the information possessed by decision-makers. In a legislative setting, we require not only that voters know the preferences of all other voters, but also that they can forecast votes in the distant future in order to choose their positions today. In election position-taking, the uncovered set solution assumes each candidate knows the utility functions of the voters and from them each candidate can calculate the uncovered set. If these information conditions are unreasonable, then the move in the direction of an incomplete-information model ought to be considered. Lupia and McCubbins (1997) note that if the act of voting is costly and the participants are unsure about the preferences of others before a vote and the utility of policy after adoption, then legislators might not hold votes at all (see also Sloss, 1973). The effect of uncertainty has also been investigated in models of elections. If voter preferences are privately held, for example, the best a candidate can do is to build a probability model of what the voter is likely to do on the basis of available information. If the voter is treated in this way, one arrives at a model known as "probabilistic voting." Hinich (1977) showed that when voters are viewed as probability processes, then competitive majority rule position-taking by candidates leads to the mean, not the median of voter ideal points. Extensions of the probabilistic voting model are considered in Coughlin (1992). The main result of probabilistic models is that outcomes are attracted to the mean of voter ideal points. In contrast, Glazer, Grofman, and Owen (1989) showed that when an incumbent office-holder's position is already known to the voters, the challenger will move closer to the incumbent, even if the incumbent is not in the center of the space.

7. CONCLUSION: LOOKING BACKWARD AND FORWARD

This book has focused on the methodology and research questions of social choice theory. Although social choice has its roots in the distant past, it is still a comparatively young field of study. For a young field, there is an astonishing (bewildering?) array of models and results. This book has, without apology, picked through a large number of important studies, emphasizing some results and completely ignoring others. That strategy was pursued in order to maintain focus and organization, even as some vital areas of study are overlooked. In this concluding chapter, however, some of these omissions can be addressed. As a part of the review of what has been accomplished in this volume, directions for further study can be emphasized.

The birth of modern social choice theory took place in the late 1940s and early 1950s, when luminaries like Kenneth Arrow and Duncan Black began their work. Arrow's research started the field in a normative direction, evaluating voting methods in the hope of finding a solution to the general (im)possibility theorem. A number of authors have tried to find a way to slightly alter the Arrow conditions in order to solve the apparent contradiction, but these attempts have not succeeded. For each weakening of an assumption, a slight strengthening of another can cause the contradiction to re-emerge (Kelly, 1978).

Since the theorem proves that there is no perfect method of voting that suits all problems and preference profiles, one logical research strategy is to try to find procedures that are acceptable for certain problems. There is a lively research area concerning the appealing properties of various methods of voting. Riker (1958, 1961), one of the first political scientists to see the importance of Arrow's theorem, offered an elegant and thorough treatment of issues concerning methods of voting in his book *Liberalism against Populism* [Riker, 1982; see also the symposium edited by Levin and Nalebuff (1995)].

One implication of Arrow's theorem, which was pointed out in research by Gibbard (1973) and Satterthwaite (1975), is that voters will sometimes be inclined to lie about their preferences, no matter what method of voting is used. Strategic voting cannot be eliminated by the design of a political system, in other words. For any procedure, it is always possible to find a profile in which at least one voter will prefer to lie or "misreport" his or her preferences. One might have expected as much, of course. From the study of multidimensional decision-making, we know that an agenda-setter can lead sincere voters from any point to any other. A voter with sophisticated foresight can certainly curb an agenda-setter. These findings focus on the possibility, not the ease or practicality, of manipulating an election. It is interesting to look at this from a computational point of view, to try to measure the number of calculations that one might need to make in order to affect an election? The reader could pursue this topic by investigating the work of Bartholdi, Tovey, and Trick (1992), who ask "how hard is it to control an election?" and offer a provocative answer.

Another troublesome implication of Arrow's theorem does not apply to whole societies, but rather to the individual. Arrow and Raynaud (1986), in their book *Social Choice and Multicriterion Decision-Making*, interpret the theorem as it applies to a single person. Instead of thinking of the inputs $(R_1, R_2, \ldots, R_n)$ as representing the rankings of many different voters, suppose they are instead rankings of alternatives created by a single person by applying different criteria. For example, a car buyer can rank the alternatives by their color, motor, wheels, gas mileage, and so forth. The question is this: can an individual condense these many rankings into an overall ranking that allows a rational choice? The individual process of compiling these items into a ranking may be formal or informal, but from Arrow's theorem we know that there is something problematic about it. It may be that a person who rigidly applies a method of comparison to a set of alternatives could cycle through them. One might think, "the Chevy is better than the Ford on five of nine dimensions, the Toyota is better than the Chevy, but the Chevy is better than the Toyota." In other words, if a person follows a scheme for making an "organized, rational plan of action," then that person might end up with intransitive preferences. The implications of this idea deserve further investigation.

The spatial model can be thought of as an enrichment of the set of admissible alternatives. Rather than investigating the choice from a discrete set (such as $\{x, y, z\}$ in Arrow's theorem), the spatial model allows the alternatives to be drawn from a segment of the real number line or a multidimensional space. One of the points of emphasis in the study of the one-dimensional model is that the incoherence of social decision—cycles—is eliminated if the voter preferences are single-peaked. The equilibrium point, as indicated by the median voter theorem, is the median of the most-preferred points of the voters. This result has been fundamental in a great many studies of electoral position-taking by candidates and legislative decisions. One of the interesting questions is whether including policy-oriented candidates, who seek not only to win an election but also to implement their favorite policies after they are elected, will significantly change the dynamics of the model (Calvert, 1985; Harrington, 1992).

Studies of the multidimensional spatial model led to the conclusion that majority rule might cycle through the set of alternatives. Optimism about coherence of multidimensional social choice was crushed by results showing the fragility of majority rule equilibrium points and the chaos theorems. By the late 1970s, it was recognized that the happy conclusion of the one-dimensional model, the median voter theorem, does not carry over to models of many dimensions. If a voting body is to select alternatives that are multifaceted, and we expect that they often do, the conclusions of the majority rule chaos theory are most discouraging. No equilibrium point is likely to exist, and under those conditions, majority rule can wander virtually anywhere.

The fact that majority rule can wander does not mean that it will, of course. It might be that voters are smart enough to block an agenda-setter who seeks to lead them from point *a* to point *b*. If voters don't want to end up at point *b*, all they have to do is vote "no" when they are asked to reject point *a*. If the trajectory is killed at the first step, there can be no wandering majority. The interesting question, of course, is whether voters do have this kind of foresight and whether they are, in fact, able to follow through on a plan to block an agenda-setter. At least one study has argued that strategic voting is unlikely in Congress because it is costly for legislators to lie about their preferences. The hometown voters may not understand strategic behavior and might punish their representative for voting against their interests (Denzau, Riker, and Shepsle, 1985).

Much of the perceived stability of policy in a multidimensional world flows, not from the preferences of the voters, but from procedures that restrict voting. If someone has the power to say, "that's it! Voting is finished," then the full extent of the majority rule cycle is not observed. This, of course, is the simplest possible structure-induced equilibrium. A rich interaction between scholars who study

Congressional politics and social choice theorists has led to a very productive field of study. Why are institutions created and what effects do they have on decision-making? The richness of this field of study is seen quite clearly in vigorous research on the nature and importance of the Congressional committee system.

The social choice theories have a broader reach, of course. While the original results were aimed at institutions that seemed particularly American, such as two-candidate elections under majority rule or committee systems in Congress, there is now interest in a broad variety of institutions that can be found around the world. There are systems of government that use different methods of electing candidates, for example. Most notable are multicandidate elections that use proportional representation or the single nontransferrable vote to choose a slate of winners. These systems differ in significant ways from single-member district elections (Shepsle, 1991; Cox, 1987b; Monroe, 1995). Some systems have a one house legislature and use a parliamentary system to choose executive officials (Laver and Schofield, 1990; Shepsle, 1994; Austen-Smith and Banks, 1990; Laver and Shepsle, 1990; Strom, 1994). Decision-making in international bodies, such as the United Nations or the European Union, can be investigated (Tsebelis, 1994).

In studies of political structures, whether they are in U.S. or foreign governments, the United Nations, voluntary organizations, or corporate board rooms, the fundamental questions are the same. The aim is to understand the outcomes of political decision-making processes as a result of the interaction of individual behavior with political institutions. Active research into the effects of institutions on political outcomes and representation will no doubt continue. At the same time, there is growing interest in questions about the formation of institutions themselves (e.g., Shepsle, 1986; North, 1990; Knight, 1992; Grafstein, 1992; Humes, 1993). Studies of institutional formation touch on some of the most important and long-standing questions in social science. Are institutions designed with foresight of (or in anticipation of) the effects they will have on political outcomes? Why are some institutions stable over the long run, while others are frequently altered?

A student who wants to pursue these questions should track down some of these studies. The mathematical notation may differ across projects, but the central tools of social choice—preferences, equilibrium, institutions—will be familiar. After an examination of the substance at hand—after finding an interesting topic—it may be necessary to investigate new methods. The next step is probably going to be into the theory of games, the study of strategic interaction among people who are (more or less) aware of their effects on their environment and other people. The recent volume by Fink, Gates, and Humes (1998), will provide some helpful guidance.

REFERENCES

ARROW, K. (1951) *Social Choice and Individual Values*. New York: Wiley. pp. 97–100.

ARROW, K. A. (1963) *Social Choice and Individual Values*. 2nd ed. New York: Wiley.

ARROW, K. J., and RAYNAUD, H. (1986) *Social Choice and Multicriterion Decision-Making*. Cambridge, MA: MIT Press.

AUSTEN-SMITH, D., and BANKS, J. (1990) "Stable governments and the allocation of policy portfolios." *American Political Science Review, 84*, 891–906.

BANKS, J. S. (1985) "Sophisticated voting outcomes and agenda control." *Social Choice and Welfare 1*, 295–306.

BARTHOLDI, J. J., TOVEY, C. A., and TRICK, M. A. (1992) "How hard is it to control an election?" *Mathematical and Computer Modelling, 16*, 27–40.

BLACK, D. (1958) *The Theory of Committees and Elections*. Cambridge: Cambridge University Press.

BLACK, D., and NEWING, R. A. (1951) *Committee Decisions with Complementary Valuation*. London: William Hodge.

BLAU, J. H. (1972) "A direct proof of Arrow's theorem." *Econometrica, 40*, 61–67.

BUCHANAN, J. M., and TULLOCK, G. (1962) *The Calculus of Consent*. Ann Arbor: University of Michigan Press.

CALVERT, R. (1985) "Robustness of the multidimensional voting model: Candidate motivations, uncertainty, and convergence." *American Journal of Political Science, 29*, 69–95.

CAPLIN, A., and NALEBUFF, B. (1988) "On 64%-majority rule." *Econometrica, 56*, 787–814.

CAPLIN, A., and NALEBUFF, B. (1991) "Aggregation and social choice: A mean voter theorem." *Econometrica, 59*, 1–24.

COUGHLIN, P. (1992) *Probabilistic Voting Theory*. New York: Cambridge University Press.

COX, G. (1987a) "The uncovered set and the core." *American Journal of Political Science, 31*, 408–423.

COX, G. (1987b) "Electoral equilibrium under alternative voting institutions." *American Journal of Political Science, 31*, 82–108.

DAVIS, O. A., and HINICH, M. J. (1966) "A mathematical model of policy formation in a democratic society," In J. L. Bernd (ed.), *Mathematical Applications in Political Science II*. Dallas: Southern Methodist University Press.

DAVIS, O. A., and HINICH, M. J. (1967) "Some results related to a mathematical model of policy formation in a democratic society." In J. L. Bernd (ed.), *Mathematical Applications in Political Science III*. Charlottesville: University of Virginia Press.

DAVIS, O., DEGROOT, M., and HINICH, M. (1972) "Social preference orderings and majority rule." *Econometrica, 40*, 147–157.

DAVIS, O. A., HINICH, M. J., and ORDESHOOK, P. C. (1970) "An expository development of a mathematical model of the political process." *American Political Science Review, 64*, 426–448.

DEBREU, G. (1959) *Theory of Value*. New Haven, CT: Yale University Press.

DENZAU, A. T., and MACKAY, R. J. (1981) "Structure induced equilibrium and perfect foresight expectations." *American Journal of Political Science, 25*, 762–779.

DENZAU, A. T., and MACKAY, R. J. (1983) "Gatekeeping and monopoly power of committees." *American Journal of Political Science, 27,* 740–761.

DENZAU, A. T., RIKER, W. H., and SHEPSLE, K. A. (1985) "Farquharson and Fenno: Sophisticated voting and home style." *American Political Science Review, 79,* 1117–1134.

DION, D., and HUBER, J. (1996) "Procedural choice and the House Committee on Rules." *Journal of Politics, 57,* 25–53.

DODGSON, C. L. (1958) "A method of taking votes on more than two issues." In D. Black (ed.), *Theory of Committees and Elections.* Cambridge, UK: Cambridge University Press. (Essay originally published in 1876.)

DOWNS, A. (1957) *An Economic Theory of Democracy.* New York: Harper and Row.

ENELOW, J., and HINICH, M. (1983a) "On Plott's pairwise symmetry condition for majority rule equilibrium." *Public Choice, 40,* 317–321.

ENELOW, J., and HINICH, M. (1983b) "Voting one issue at a time: The question of voter forecasts." *American Political Science Review, 77,* 435–445.

ENELOW, J., and HINICH, M. (1984a) *The Spatial Theory of Voting: An Introduction.* Cambridge, UK: Cambridge University Press.

ENELOW, J., and HINICH, M. (1984b) "A generalized model of voting one issue at a time with applications to Congress." *American Journal of Political Science, 28,* 587–597.

EPPLE, D., and KADANE, J. B. (1990) "Sequential voting with endogenous voter forecasts," *American Political Science Review, 84,* 165–176.

FARQUHARSON, R. (1969) *Theory of Voting.* New Haven, CT: Yale University Press.

FELD, S. L., and GROFMAN, B. (1987) "Necessary and sufficient conditions for a majority winner in *n*-dimensional spatial voting games: An intuitive geometric approach." *American Journal of Political Science, 31,* 709–728.

FELD, S. L., GROFMAN, B., and MILLER, N. R. (1989) "Limits on agenda control in spatial voting games." *Mathematical and Computer Modelling, 12,* 405–416.

FINK, E. C., GATES, S., and HUMES, B. D. (1998) *Game Theory Topics: Incomplete Information, Repeated Games, and N-Player Games.* Sage University Paper Series on Quantitative Applications in the Social Sciences, 07-122. Thousand Oaks, California: Sage Publications.

FISHBURN, P. C. (1973) *The Theory of Social Choice.* Princeton, NJ: Princeton University Press.

GIBBARD, A. (1973) "Manipulation of voting schemes: A general result." *Econometrica, 41,* 587–602.

GILLIGAN, T. W., and KREHBIEL, K. (1987) "Collective decision-making and standing committees: An informational rationale for restrictive amendment procedures." *Journal of Law, Economics, and Organization, 3,* 287–335.

GLAZER, A., GROFMAN, B., and OWEN, G. (1989) *Mathematical and Computer Modelling, 12,* 471–478.

GRAFSTEIN, R. (1992) *Institutional Realism: Social and Political Constraints on Rational Actors.* New Haven, CT: Yale University Press.

GREENBERG, J. (1979) "Consistent majority rules over compact sets of alternatives." *Econometrica, 47,* 627–636.

GROSECLOSE, T. (1994) "Testing committee composition hypotheses for the U.S. Congress." *Journal of Politics, 56,* 440–458.

HAMMOND, T. H., and MILLER, G. J. (1987) "The core of the Constitution." *American Political Science Review, 81,* 1155–1174.

HARRINGTON, J. (1992) "The revelation of information through the electoral process: An exploratory analysis." *Economics and Politics, 4,* 225-276.

HINICH, M. (1977) "The median voter result is an artifact." *Journal of Economic Theory, 16,* 208-219.

HINICH, M., and MUNGER, M. (1994) *Ideology and the Theory of Political Choice.* Ann Arbor: University of Michigan Press.

HOTELLING, H. (1929) "Stability in competition." *Economic Journal, 39,* 41-57.

HUMES, B. D. (1993) "Majority rule outcomes and the choice of germaneness rules." *Public Choice, 75,* 301-317.

INGBERMAN, D., and YAO, D. (1991) "Presidential commitment and the veto." *American Journal of Political Science, 35,* 357-389.

JOHNSON, P. E. (1990) "Unraveling in democratically governed groups." *Rationality and Society, 2,* 4-34.

JOHNSON, P. E. (1996) "Unraveling in a variety of institutional settings." *Journal of Theoretical Politics, 8,* 299-331.

JONES, B., RADCLIFF, B., TABER, C., and TIMPONE, R. (1995) "Condorcet winners and the paradox of voting: Probability calculations for weak preference orders." *American Political Science Review, 89,* 137-144.

KADANE, J. B. (1972) "On division of the question." *Public Choice, 13,* 47-54.

KELLY, J. S. (1978) *Arrow Impossibility Theorems.* New York: Academic Press.

KIEWIET, D. R., and McCUBBINS, M. D. (1988) "Presidential influence on Congressional appropriations decisions." *American Journal of Political Science, 32,* 713-736.

KNIGHT, J. (1992) *Institutions and Social Conflict.* Cambridge, U.K.: Cambridge University Press.

KRAMER, G. H. (1972) "Sophisticated voting over multidimensional choice spaces." *Journal of Mathematical Sociology, 2,* 165-180.

KREHBIEL, K. (1991) *Institutions and Legislative Organization.* Ann Arbor: University of Michigan Press.

KREHBIEL, K. (1997) "Restrictive rules reconsidered." *American Journal of Political Science, 41,* 919-944.

KREPS, D. (1990) *A Course in Microeconomic Theory.* Princeton: Princeton University Press.

LAVER, M., and SCHOFIELD, N. (1990) *Multiparty Government: The Politics of Coalition in Europe.* New York: Oxford University Press.

LAVER, M., and SHEPSLE, K. A. (1990) "Coalitions and cabinet government." *American Political Science Review, 84,* 873-890.

LEDYARD, J. O. (1981) "The paradox of voting and candidate competition: A general equilibrium analysis." In G. Horwich and J. Quirk (eds.), *Essays in the Contemporary Fields of Economics,* pp. 54-80. West Lafayette, IN: Purdue University Press.

LEDYARD, J. O. (1984) "The pure theory of large two candidate elections." *Public Choice, 44,* 7-41.

LEVIN, J., and NALEBUFF, B. (1995) "An introduction to vote-counting schemes." *Journal of Economic Perspectives, 9,* 3-26.

LUPIA, A., and McCUBBINS, M. D. (1997) "On the stability of social choice: Scarcity, uncertainty, and the barriers to change." University of California, San Diego, unpublished.

MAY, K. O. (1952) "A set of independent necessary and sufficient conditions for simple majority decision." *Econometrica, 20*, 680–684.

McCUBBINS, M. D., and SULLIVAN, T. (1987) *Congress: Structure and Policy.* Cambridge: Cambridge University Press.

McKELVEY, R. D. (1976) "Intransitivities in multidimensional voting models and some implications for agenda control." *Journal of Economic Theory, 12*, 472–482.

McKELVEY, R. D. (1986) "Covering, dominance, and institution-free properties of social choice." *American Journal of Political Science, 30*, 283–314.

McKELVEY, R. D. (1990) "Game theoretic models of voting in multidimensional issue spaces." In T. Ichiishi et al. (Eds.), *Game Theory and Applications.* San Diego: Academic Press.

McKELVEY, R. D., and NIEMI, R. G. (1978) "A multistage game representation of sophisticated voting for binary procedures." *Journal of Economic Theory, 18*, 1–22.

McKELVEY, R. D., and SCHOFIELD, N. (1987) "Generalized symmetry conditions at a core point." *Econometrica, 55*, 923–933.

MILLER, N. (1980) "A new solution set for tournaments and majority voting." *American Journal of Political Science, 24*, 68–96.

MILLER, N. (1995) *Committees, Agendas, and Voting.* Chur, Switzerland: Harwood.

MONROE, B. (1995) "Fully proportional representation." *American Political Science Review, 89*, 925–940.

NORTH, D. C. (1990) *Institutions, Institutional Change, and Economic Performance,* Cambridge, UK: Cambridge University Press.

ORDESHOOK, P. C. (1986) *Game Theory and Political Theory: An Introduction.* Cambridge: Cambridge University Press.

ORDESHOOK, P. C., and SCHWARTZ, T. (1987) "Agendas and the control of political outcomes." *American Political Science Review, 81*, 179–200.

PALFREY, T. R. (1984) "Spatial equilibrium with entry." *Review of Economic Studies, 51*, 139–156.

PLOTT, C. R. (1967) "A notion of equilibrium and its possibility under majority rule." *American Economic Review, 57*, 787–806.

POOLE, K. T. (1997) "Changing minds? Not in Congress!" Working Paper. Available on the World Wide Web at http://wizard.ucr.edu/polmeth/working_papers97/poole97a.html.

PUN, W. (1997) "Majority voting with bribes does not eliminate voting cycles." *Journal of Theoretical Politics, 9*, 131–134.

RIKER, W. H. (1958) "The paradox of voting and Congressional rules for voting on amendments." *American Political Science Review, 52*, 349–366.

RIKER, W. H. (1961) "Voting and the summation of preferences." *American Political Science Review, 55*, 900–911.

RIKER, W. H. (1982) *Liberalism against Populism: A Confrontation between the Theory of Democracy and the Theory of Social Choice.* San Francisco: W. H. Freeman.

ROMER, T., and ROSENTHAL, H. (1978) "Political resource allocation, controlled agendas, and the status quo." *Public Choice, 33*, 27–44.

ROSENTHAL, H. (1990) "The setter model." In J. M. Enelow and M. J. Hinich (Eds.), *Advances in the Spatial Theory of Voting.* Cambridge, UK: Cambridge University Press.

106

SATTERTHWAITE, M. (1975) "Strategy-proofness and Arrow's conditions: Existence and correspondence theorems for voting procedures and social welfare functions." *Journal of Economic Theory, 10,* 187–218.

SCHOFIELD, N. (1978a) "Instability of simple dynamic games." *Review of Economic Studies, 45,* 575–594.

SCHOFIELD, N. (1978b) "Generic instability of voting games." Presented at the Annual Meetings of the Public Choice Society, New Orleans.

SCHOFIELD, N. (1980) "Generic properties of simple Bergson–Samuelson welfare functions." *Journal of Mathematical Economics, 7,* 175–192.

SCHOFIELD, N. (1983) "Generic instability of majority rule." *Review of Economic Studies, 50,* 695–705.

SCHOFIELD, N. (1994) "The C^1 topology on the space of preference profiles and the existence of a continuous preference aggregation." School of Business and Center in Political Economy, Washington University in St. Louis, unpublished.

SCHWARTZ, T. (1977) "Collective choice, separation of issues and vote trading." *American Political Science Review, 71,* 999–1010.

SCHWARTZ, T. (1981) "The universal impossibility theorem." *Public Choice, 37,* 487–501.

SCHWARTZ, T. (1986) *The Logic of Collective Choice.* New York: Columbia University Press.

SEN, A. K. (1970) *Collective Choice and Social Welfare.* London: Holden-Day.

SHEPSLE, K. A. (1979) "Institutional arrangements and equilibrium in multidimensional voting models." *American Journal of Political Science, 23,* 27–59.

SHEPSLE, K. A. (1986) "Institutional equilibrium and equilibrium institutions." In H. F. Weisberg (Ed.), *Political Science: The Science of Politics.* New York: Agathon Press.

SHEPSLE, K. A. (1991) *Models of Multiparty Electoral Competition.* Chur, Switzerland: Harwood Press.

SHEPSLE, K. A. (1994) *Cabinet Ministers and Parliamentary Government.* New York: Cambridge University Press.

SHEPSLE, K. A., and WEINGAST, B. R. (1981) "Structure-induced equilibrium and legislative choice." *Public Choice, 37,* 503–519.

SHEPSLE, K. A., and WEINGAST, B. (1984) "Uncovered sets and sophisticated voting outcomes with implications for agenda institutions." *American Journal of Political Science, 28,* 49–74.

SLOSS, J. (1973) "Stable outcomes in majority voting games." *Public Choice, 15,* 19–48.

SLUTSKY, S. (1979) "Equilibrium under α-majority voting." *Econometrica, 47,* 1113–1124.

SMITHIES, A. (1941) "Optimum location in spatial competition." *Journal of Political Economy, 49,* 423–439.

STOKES, D. E. (1963) "Spatial models of party competition." *American Political Science Review, 57,* 368–377.

STROM, K. (1994) "The Presthus debacle: Intraparty politics and bargaining failure in Norway." *American Political Science Review, 88,* 112–127.

TSEBELIS, G. (1994) "The power of the European parliament as a conditional agenda setter." *American Political Science Review, 88,* 128–142.